Contents ○ ● ○ ○

Notes on Contributors

Belle Wallace has worked with very able children for 25 years: first in an advisory capacity to Essex schools; and then as a researcher and developer of a problem-solving and thinking skills base for curriculum development. She is currently President of NACE (The National Association for Able Children in Education) and editor of *Gifted Education International*, a triannual journal which has been published since 1982 by AB Academic Publishers, Oxford. Belle has served on the Executive Committee of the World Council for Gifted and Talented Children (WCGTC), has published widely and given keynote lectures nationally and internationally. She has two major interests: first, identifying and developing the potential of disadvantaged children; and, secondly, developing teachers' expertise in using problem-solving and thinking skills strategies in the classroom.

Nicola Beverley has been a Curriculum Advisor for Primary Science in Lincolnshire for five years. She provides support to schools in the overall development of the science curriculum, and also to individual teachers seeking to extend their personal knowledge and understanding in science, together with their classroom management skills. As an active member of the Association for Science Education (section and regional commit-

Teaching Thinking Skills Across the Early Years

A practical approach for children aged 4–7

Belle Wallace

with Nicola Beverley,

Mike Carter, Lynne McClure

and Dorothy Rickarby

David Fulton Publishers

London

In association with

The National Association for Able Children in Education

Other titles in the series:

Using History to Develop Thinking Skills at Key Stage 2
Belle Wallace and Peter Riches

Using Science to Develop Thinking Skills at Key Stage 3
Pat O'Brien

Teaching Thinking Skills Across the Middle Years
Belle Wallace and Richard Bentley

Teaching Thinking Skills Across the Primary Curriculum
Belle Wallace

Teaching Skills and Early Childhood Education
Patrick J.M. Costello

David Fulton Publishers Ltd
The Chiswick Centre, 414 Chiswick High Road, London W4 5TF

www.fultonpublishers.co.uk

First published in Great Britain by David Fulton Publishers 2002
10 9 8 7 6 5 4 3

British Library Cataloguing in Publication Data
A catalogue record for this book is available from the British Library.

ISBN 1–85346–842–8

Typeset by FiSH Books, London
Printed and bound in Great Britain by Thanet Press.

tees) she is actively involved in raising the profile of science throughout the East Midlands.

Mike Carter is a freelance educational consultant and trainer. For ten years he was an LEA and OFSTED Inspector. Prior to that he was a headteacher of an Infant School and then a First School. Mike has also worked for a time in initial teacher training. He is currently working with 22 schools in the Worcester and Kidderminster Education Achievement Zones as a monitor and evaluator.

Lynne McClure's passion for mathematics has led her to teach across all ages and abilities, including initial teacher education, secondary and primary teaching and adult basic numeracy. For several years she combined primary teaching with teacher training but took time out to educate each of her four daughters at home. Most recently, Lynne has worked in the Research Centre for Able Pupils at Oxford Brookes University where she had the opportunity to pursue research into how very able young children think about mathematics.

Dorothy Rickarby is headteacher of a Primary School with 4 classes and she teaches a mixed Year 5/6 class for part of the week. She trained as a mature student in Liverpool and began teaching in Toxteth. Dorothy has worked in a variety of schools in Liverpool and Worcestershire before taking up her current post five years ago.

Acknowledgements

My special thanks to Harvey B. Adams, since we worked together over many years to research a generic and educationally sound theoretical framework for the development of problem-solving and thinking skills across the curriculum. I am grateful for the hours of discussion spent in the re-formulation of ideas and for the energy used in trialling ideas and strategies in diverse classrooms around the world.

My thanks also to Nicola Beverley, Mike Carter, Lynne McClure and Dorothy Rickarby for their expertise and their willingness to spend many hours devising and trialling their ideas in classrooms. A theoretical framework about how children best learn is only useful if it generates good practice, and the co-writers have contributed ideas with the reality of the classroom in the forefront of their minds.

Thanks, too, to the following headteachers and classroom teachers who have been members of the wider school groups: they have trialled ideas and supported the writers by being so willing to spend extra hours in preparation and evaluative discussion. Their love for and commitment to the children in their care is indicative of their dedication and their professionalism.

Barrowby CE Primary School, Lincs: Sylvia West (Headteacher), Natalie Bannister, Kath Lee, Shelley Tinkley

Gonerby Hill Foot CE Primary School, Lincs: Peter Riches (Headteacher), Rachel Bensley, Lisa Gordon

Harrowby CE Infant School: Fiona Griffiths (Headteacher), Susan Hayward, Paula Westwood

Little Gonerby CE Infant School, Lincs: Elizabeth Wiggins (Headteacher), Emma Jacklin, Helen Tansey, Marguerite Tibbett, Terry Beese

Peartree Nursery Unit and Reception, Sidemoor First School and Nursery, Bromsgrove, Worcs: with grateful thanks to Lesley Leigh (Headteacher). Special thanks to Anne Taylor, Nursery Teacher and Early Years Coordinator at Sidemoor First School and Nursery for the photographs she contributed that are used throughout the book.

St Mary's RC Primary School, Boston, Lincs: Katherine Doherty (Headteacher), Janice Carder

Stickney Primary School, Lincs: Chris Holmes (Headteacher), Helen Challinor

The Tedder Primary School, Lincs: Christine Reeve (Headteacher), Sue Staniland

Wootton St Peter's Primary School, Abingdon, Oxford: thanks to the Headteacher and teachers, with special thanks to Tricia Kraftl

Belle Wallace
June 2002

○●○○ Preface

The following portrait of Thomas is taken from Gervase Phinn's *Over Hill and Dale* (extracts from pp. 48–50), published by Michael Joseph Ltd (2000).

I was feeling confident and pleased with myself when I appeared after morning playtime in the classroom of Mrs Dunne. I gathered the small children around me on the carpet in the Reading Corner and we talked about several large colour photographs of various animals which I had brought with me. I explained that we were going to write some little descriptive poems about the different creatures which included a mole, rabbit, squirrel and dormouse...

A large round child called Thomas, remarked casually that his grandad killed moles.

'Does he really?' I replied casually and attempted to move on. 'Now look at his fat little black body. He's an unusual little creature, the mole. Can you see his big flat paws like spades and the sharp claws? Can anyone tell me what –'

'They dig and dig wi' them claws, deep underground they go and chuck up reight big mounds of soil,' explained Thomas to no one in particular. 'Do a lot o' damage to a field, do moles. They're a real pest my grandad says. Some farmers put down poison but me grandad traps 'em and hangs up their bodies on t' fence.'

I decided to look at another picture. 'Here we have a grey squirrel. I saw a squirrel this morning peeping from between the branches of a tree outside. Look at his large black eyes and long bushy tail. Can anyone tell me what –'

'Tree vermin', commented the same little boy. 'My grandad shoots them an' all. Ruin trees, they do. My grandad says squirrels are a damn nuisance. They eat all t'corn put out for t'hens. Rats wi' bushy tails, that's what squirrels are. My grandad goes out in t'morning with his shotgun, shoots 'em and hangs up their bodies on t'fence.'

'Just listen a moment, will you, Thomas...'

'We can perhaps talk about that later on. Now I want us all to look very carefully at this picture of a rabbit...'

'My grandad kills them an' all,' said Thomas. 'He pegs a little string net ovver t'rabbit warren holes and lets one of his jills down.'

'Jills?' I asked.

'His ferret. He keeps her half fed to make her keen. If he underfeeds her, she eats t'rabbit and won't come up out of t'ole. If he overfeeds her she won't go down at all. He lets her down t'hole and she chases t'rabbits out into t'net. Then my grandad breaks their necks. He's reight good at that.'...

'And what about dormice, Thomas? Does your grandad kill those as well and hang them up on the fence?'

'No, he quite likes dormice. They don't really do any harm.'...

'Sheba kills dormice, though,' said Thomas in his flat, matter-of-fact voice.

'Sheba?' I sighed.

'Our farm cat. She catches 'em in t'fields, carries 'em into t'kitchen and plays with 'em before killing 'em. We try to get 'em off of 'er but she runs off.'

'I see,' I said wearily.

'And sometimes she brings shrews into t'kitchen an' all, and bites their 'eads off and – '

'Is there anyone else who would like to say anything about animals?' I interrupted, in the hope of changing the subject. A small pixie-faced little boy sitting right under my nose raised his hand eagerly.

'Yes?' I said pleasantly, looking into his keen little face. 'What have you got to tell me?'

'I've got frogs on my underpants,' he announced proudly.

By the end of the morning the children had produced some short interesting poems about the animals. Most were not about little, soft-furred moles, adorable little dormice, gambolling rabbits or playful squirrels but were blunt, realistic descriptions of the animals that they knew so much about – far more than ever I would. . . .

Thomas's effort was quite clearly the best:

On a frosty morning, my grandad
Takes his jill to catch rabbits.
She has a little blue collar and a silver bell,
Tiny red eyes and creamy fur,
And she trembles in his hands.

For Teachers, Parents and Children

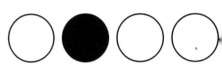

The human mind is amazing! It is a mystery! Often thoughts come and we wonder where from: from some memorable experience or deep impression, from interaction with another person, or just from a kaleidoscope of responses triggered through our senses. We are a wonderful combination of all our intelligences: linguistic, logical/mathematical, spatial/visual, bodily kinaesthetic, social, personal and spiritual.

As adults, we are often unsure of what we really think, how we will respond or how we feel about certain things: we are even less sure when we try to interpret how other people think and feel. How then can the mind be measured or quantified? As teachers and parents in care of the young, how can we rank and grade children in order? At best we can only measure a few learned skills at a point in time; we can only use our professional intuition and diagnose what young learners need before trying to respond in appropriate ways.

How then can we know what children are really learning? It is clear that we cannot know with any certainty. We can only provide opportunities and then trust that young children have an innate desire to learn. There are signs, however! For example, a young child who is engrossed in solving a puzzle or completing a painting; another child who is lost in daydreams in the home corner; yet another who dresses up in finery and parades the 'character'; and still another who builds a complex, magical structure from bits and pieces.

So do we just stand by and let learning happen? For some of the time, yes we do. But we also need to interact with questions and talking to open up new avenues, to develop language, to teach relevant skills and to model ways of working. However, when we model to children we not only need to model behaviour and ways of doing things efficiently; we must also model thinking and problem-solving. We need to share our thinking strategies while allowing children to discover and experiment with their own. It is a delicate balance achieved by skilled teachers – when to allow discovery, when to prompt and guide, and when to teach directly the skills that learners need for efficient learning.

The greatest gift teachers and parents can give to children is the gift of learning how to learn. So we need to allow children to learn as much as they can through interest, curiosity, experience and excitement; we then need to weave into this tapestry the skills children need for further learning. The most important skills revolve around identifying problems in the first place, deriving a range of possible strategies to resolve them, solving them as well as possible, then reviewing the whole thinking procedure to refine and crystallise the procedures ready for the next time.

Quoting from a case study of a young child:

> The small boy had obviously got up early to go about his important business. There were scurrying sounds coming from his room but stuck to the closed door was the sign:
>
> 'Do not distobe. I am very bizy. I wil call you wen I need you.'
>
> The scurrying went on for about an hour. Then the small boy, still in his pyjamas, tumbled downstairs. Breathlessly he said:
>
> 'Right! It's all ready. Can you help me write the notices? I want to start my own play group and I've organised all the games.'
>
> The seven year old was flushed with excitement. He had indeed organised his small room into clusters of toys and bits of paper and crayons and paint and Lego. It was a treasure trove of possibilities.
>
> 'I just need you to be the grownup who looks after us', he proudly announced.

**THE NATIONAL ASSOCIATION FOR
ABLE CHILDREN IN EDUCATION
NACE National Office, PO Box 242
Arnolds Way, Oxford, OX2 9FR**

Registered Charity No. 327230

Tel: 01865 861879

e-mail: info@nace.co.uk

Fax: 01865 861880

www.nace.co.uk

MISSION STATEMENT

NACE...the association of professionals, promoting and supporting the education of able, gifted and talented children and young people.

AIMS

1. To promote the fact that able, gifted and talented children and young people have particular educational needs, which must be met to realise their full potential.

2. To be proactive in promoting discussion and debate by raising appropriate issues in all education forums and through liaison with educational policy matters.

3. To encourage commitment to the personal, social and intellectual development of the whole child or young person.

4. To encourage a broad, balanced and appropriate curriculum for the able, gifted and talented.

5. To encourage the use of differentiated educational provision in the classroom through curriculum enrichment and extension.

6. To make education an enjoyable, exciting and worthwhile experience for the able, gifted and talented.

OBJECTIVES

1. To promote the development, implementation and evaluation in all schools and colleges of a coherent policy for the able, gifted and talented children and young people.

2. To provide appropriate support, resources and materials for the education of the able, gifted and talented.

3. To provide methods of identification and support to the education community.

4. To provide and facilitate appropriate initial teacher training and continuing professional development for teachers and school leaders.

5. To facilitate research activities.

The National Association for Able Children in Education

In-Service Training Provision

Our trainers can provide INSET for individual schools, clusters or partnerships of schools, LEAs and Professional Development Centres.

COST PER DAY
FROM
£400
PLUS VAT
A CHARGE OF 25p
PER MILE WILL BE MADE
FOR TRAINER'S TRAVEL
PLUS SUBSISTENCE
WHEN AN OVERNIGHT STAY
HAS BEEN NECESSARY

Did you know that 1 in 5 of your pupils is able and talented?

Call us to discuss the focus of your INSET

NACE
PO Box 242, Arnolds Way,
Oxford OX2 9FR

Tel: 01865 861879
Fax: 01865 861880

E-mail: info@nace.co.uk
www.nace.co.uk

The National Association for Able Children in Education
Registered Charity No. 327230   VAT No. 536 5807 26

Teaching Problem-solving and Thinking Skills in the Early Years: Working across the Curriculum

The earlier we start the better!

BELLE WALLACE

'We thought and we thought and we had an idea and we tried it and it didn't work!'

'So what did you do then?'

'We thought and we thought again and then Jane had an idea and we tried it and it worked!'

> (Conversation about problem-solving with a group of 4 year olds reported by Lesley Leigh)

The teachers in nursery schools, the Foundation Phase and Key Stage 1 have always taken on the responsibility of developing the basic building blocks of learning for all young children. And society takes it for granted that early years teachers will lay the bedrock of Literacy and Numeracy – and these days – the rudiments of Information and Communications Technology (ICT). Of course, parents play an important role, but far too often in our

COMMENT

rushed society, young learners arrive at school with fragmented language patterns, inadequate pre-school experience of constructive play and talk, and underdeveloped emotional and social intelligence. This makes the professional role of young children's first teachers one of critical importance – our early years teachers spend huge amounts of time advising and guiding parents, filling the huge gaps in young children's experience, developing their social skills, building youngsters' self-confidence and self-efficacy.

All other teachers from Key Stage 2 onwards, and parents too, rely heavily on early years teachers doing a good job!

And indeed they do! Working with early years teachers and watching their flexibility, their ability to tackle several jobs at once, their simultaneous attention to a variety of individual needs, their orchestration of a group of young egotistical individuals into a cohesive social group, while fostering each child's individuality, provides a superb repertoire of skills needed by all subsequent teachers!

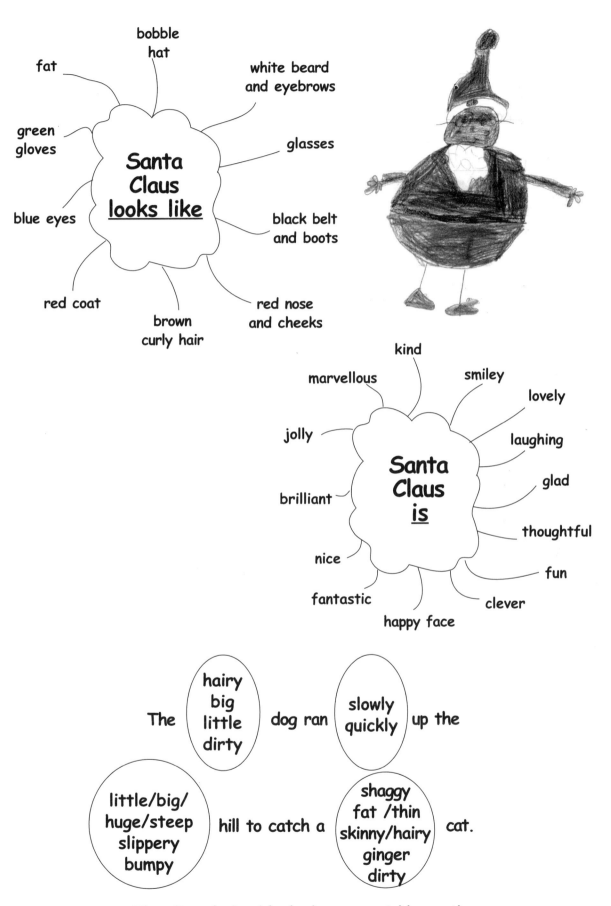

fat

bobble hat

white beard and eyebrows

green gloves

glasses

Santa Claus looks like

blue eyes

black belt and boots

red coat

brown curly hair

red nose and cheeks

kind

marvellous

smiley

lovely

jolly

laughing

Santa Claus is

brilliant

glad

thoughtful

nice

fun

fantastic

clever

happy face

The (hairy big little dirty) dog ran (slowly quickly) up the

(little/big/ huge/steep slippery bumpy) hill to catch a (shaggy fat /thin skinny/hairy ginger dirty) cat.

The dirty hairy black dog ran quickly up the slippery hill to catch a fat shaggy ginger cat.

Susan Hayward (Rec c/t) Harrowby CE Infant School (Lincs)

A skinny grey mouse ran quickly away from the fierce cat into his safe little mousehole.

Susan Hayward (Rec c/t) Harrowby CE Infant School (Lincs)

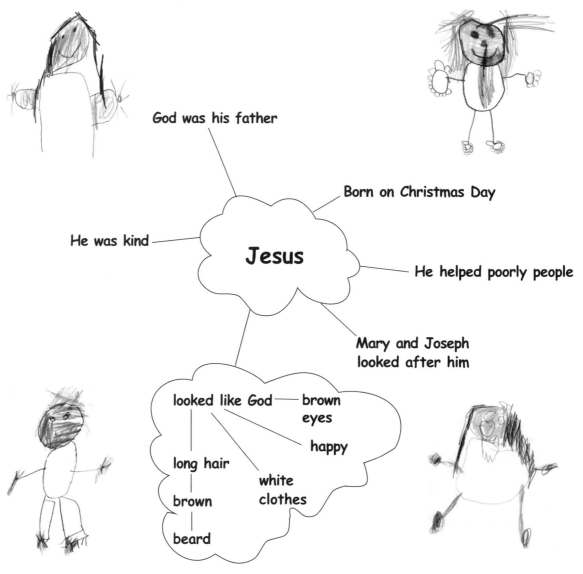

Paula Westwood (Rec c/t) Harrowby CE Infant School (Lincs)

The purpose of this chapter is not to suggest that early years teachers are not already doing a fine job, but rather to show ways of extending and consolidating their work using a coherent problem-solving and thinking skills framework. Often teachers are intuitively working within a thinking skills paradigm, but this thinking skills framework needs to be infused throughout the whole school, and it also needs to be made explicit to the children so that they become aware of what thinking skills they are using and mastering.

This chapter will present a well-researched framework for a systematic approach to the development of problem-solving and thinking skills across the curriculum; and will give examples of activities carried out in classrooms. The problem-solving framework is called TASC: Thinking Actively in a Social Context and is explained later in this chapter.

Reflect on the following comments made by teachers during staff development sessions and decide whether you agree or disagree with what's being said.

Let's think for a while about the range of skills we want children to develop.

- How important is it that the range of skills is carried across the whole curriculum?

- Has there been regular staff discussion to make sure that the children are receiving similar messages as they move from one activity to another or from one teacher to another?

- To what extent are the children aware of the thinking skills they are developing?

- Are parents aware of the skills that we, as teachers, are trying to get their children to develop?

- Have there been any training sessions held for parents?

So the purpose of this chapter is to encourage us to reflect on what we are already doing: to carry out an audit of our professional practice, and then to refine and extend that practice. In addition, we need to consider how to involve parents as much as possible since when home and school work together, the benefit for the children is enormously more effective.

We need to work firstly on social skills, in many instances even teaching children how to play!

We already have so much to cope with! Is this another new initiative?

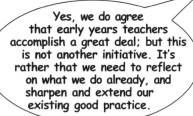

Indeed! The skills of cooperating and sharing through play are essentially important and lay the foundation for cooperative thinking and problem-solving.

Yes, we do agree that early years teachers accomplish a great deal; but this is not another initiative. It's rather that we need to reflect on what we do already, and sharpen and extend our existing good practice.

Then we have to lay the foundations of literacy and numeracy. This is often a very difficult task these days since so many children are used to quick-fix entertainment on television and video.

Many children have difficulties with language – not just children who are learning in their second language but children who are learning in their home language.

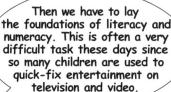

We agree. So many children are used to being entertained and have learned to be passive rather than actively involved in an activity. It's not an easy task, but we need to train young learners to be active participants in the creation of ideas and knowledge. If we can do this, we have set them well on the path of learning how to learn for themselves.

Although there are many kinds of thinking – expressing ideas through art or music, for example – we agree that language is the most important thinking tool that learners need. And learners need to develop a 'thinking language' – a repertoire of words that enables them to express thoughts.

All children need to express feelings too – frustration soon builds up and explodes when children can't say what they feel.

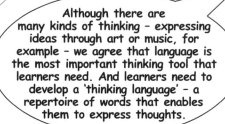

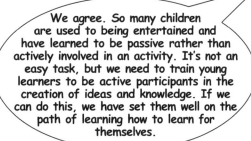

Yes, talking about feelings is the beginning of the development of emotional intelligence – the beginning of understanding the self and others. Thinking and feeling are two inseparable companions. We can't think without feeling – doing a number puzzle successfully brings great pleasure and satisfaction. Feelings colour our thoughts – feeling insecure or upset inhibits our thinking and prevents us thinking creatively or adventurously.

Some children are 'natural thinkers'; these are usually the brightest. They learn quickly and efficiently.

Surely, what happens to children in their home environment is the critical factor in fostering children's progress and development?

Sure, children have a range of genetic attributes, and a wide range of environmental experiences, but all children are capable of developing more efficient thinking skills and growing through extended experiences. As educators, we can teach children how to use a vast repertoire of thinking skills and we can constantly provide new experiences.

Certainly, we all agree that the influence of home factors on children's early experiences lay important foundations for all future learning; so it is vital that we develop parent groups based in early phase education so that, ideally, pre-school problems can be discussed and the relevant advice provided. The government must see the importance of providing funding to support this: it is so short-sighted to provide funding to alleviate problems which arise in later phases of education, when many of these problems might have been solved in the formative stages.

Is it necessary to have a consistent approach to the teaching of problem-solving and thinking skills across the curriculum? Surely, children will automatically pick up these skills?

Does this mean that all learners will all think in the same way? Where does creativity and individuality feature in all of this?

The most important factor in successful learning is that language, skills and processes are modelled to the learner. For example, the teacher thinks 'out loud', gives names or verbal labels to the skills and works in dialogue with the learners: in essence, the teacher *models* the thinking process in action while speaking the thinking language. If the modelled messages are clearly conveyed to the learners by all their teachers, the modelling is reinforced and practised until the learner absorbs and automatically uses a wide range of skills.

Every learner needs to develop a wide repertoire of basic thinking skills that they can call into use in a problem-solving situation. It's much like learning to drive a car, which consists of using a range of basic driving skills in different conditions of varying complexity. In the same way, learners need a range of language and numeracy skills that they can then use for creative problem-solving in reading, writing and mathematics.

What about learners needing to work across the range of multiple intelligences? Solving problems in art, dance, physical activities, spatial activities, music, social situations?

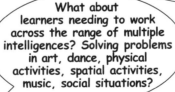

Any human activity is about using problem-solving strategies – working out a drama activity or a dance routine, building a three-dimensional structure, solving a group disagreement, or organising a party or concert. Learners need to have developed confidence in their ability to tackle a problem, have a wide range of general strategies they can identify, together with specific skills they have mastered. For example, a dancer working out a new routine needs to know how to approach the whole task, how to combine a set of movements and how to perform and improve those movements.

Theoretical background to the model of problem-solving and thinking skills used throughout this text

In the mid-1980s, Belle Wallace and Harvey B. Adams surveyed the main thinking skills packages that were in operation in various countries around the world. In many cases they visited the countries and worked with the leaders and researchers working in the field of problem-solving and thinking skills. Then adopting an eclectic approach, they combined the successful elements of all of the projects they evaluated, and conducted an intensive ten-year action research programme with groups of disadvantaged learners and their teachers. Strategies and teaching methods were trialled and refined through a cyclical process of action, evaluation, reflection, and modification that involved the students, their teachers, a group of educational psychologists and, of course, the researchers themselves. This process resulted in the development of a model for the teaching of problem-solving and thinking skills known as *TASC: Thinking Actively in a Social Context* (Wallace and Adams 1993) which sets out a framework for the development of a problem-solving and thinking skills curriculum.

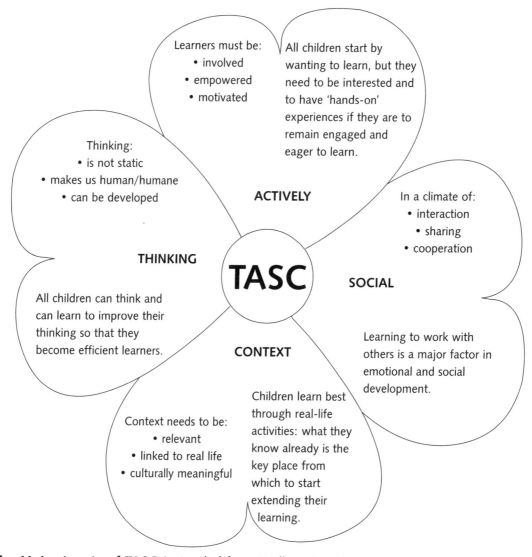

The Major tenets of TASC (extended from Wallace 2000)

Would you like to add any more to the major tenets of TASC?

The remainder of this chapter examines the TASC framework: the theoretical base, the teaching methodology and the range of core skills and strategies that should be incorporated in any programme purporting to develop a problem-solving and thinking skills approach to the curriculum. Examples of activities across the curriculum will show aspects of TASC in action in a number of classrooms.

The subsequent chapters also show TASC in action with a major focus on Literacy, Numeracy and Science: although, in early years classrooms, every opportunity is taken to work across the curriculum using a range of learning activities across the multiple intelligences. In addition, in early years classrooms, care for the social, emotional and physical development of young learners goes hand in hand with attention to their cognitive development.

The purpose of the action research programme that led to the development of TASC was to gather, trial and refine the most effective components of successful problem-solving strategies for both learners and teachers. The TASC model highlights essential elements that should be part of any thinking skills programme, but it is not a straitjacket! The TASC model is meant to be flexible and capable of modification and interpretation as long as the essential principles remain. All the contributors to this text have brought their own expertise and creativity and have applied TASC principles in their own way in a range of classrooms.

Understanding the theory that informs the base of TASC

The strength of good teachers comes from their powerful emotional and social intelligences: they can orchestrate the work of groups of children with a wide range of learning needs, while also giving attention to the individual child. Much of the diagnostic awareness of teachers stems from strong intuition and feeling, and is the result of a highly developed professional awareness of all children's needs. But as educators we also need to be able to justify the decisions we make with a sound backing of educational theory. Hence it is crucial to understand the two most important theories of how children best learn, which together form the underlying rationale from which TASC developed. The theorists may not be familiar, but the practical implications of the theories will certainly have resonance with the good practice found in classrooms.

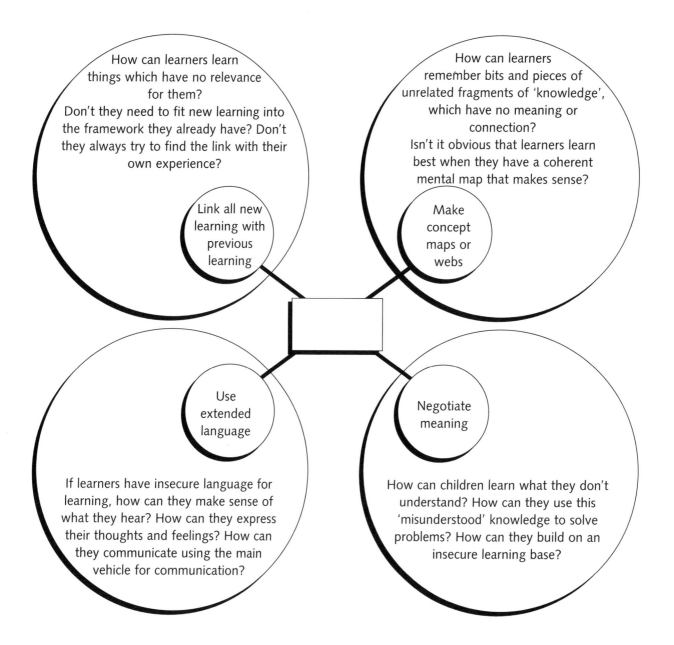

How can learners learn things which have no relevance for them?
Don't they need to fit new learning into the framework they already have? Don't they always try to find the link with their own experience?

Link all new learning with previous learning

How can learners remember bits and pieces of unrelated fragments of 'knowledge', which have no meaning or connection?
Isn't it obvious that learners learn best when they have a coherent mental map that makes sense?

Make concept maps or webs

Use extended language

If learners have insecure language for learning, how can they make sense of what they hear? How can they express their thoughts and feelings? How can they communicate using the main vehicle for communication?

Negotiate meaning

How can children learn what they don't understand? How can they use this 'misunderstood' knowledge to solve problems? How can they build on an insecure learning base?

Vygotsky's 'Development of Higher Psychological Processes' (extended from Wallace 2000)

Vygotsky (1978) shows such powerful insight into how all people – adults and children – learn. Good teachers have always known intuitively what Vygotsky is saying. Finding the 'hooks' within children's minds in order to extend into new learning is the creative artistry of every good teacher: searching out how to explain clearly, how to connect, how to make sense and reach understanding underpins the whole process of mediation. The senior learner builds the scaffolding of support until the young learner can stand independently: this is the aim of early learning. The major tool for communication and learning is language, which first needs to accommodate the child's home language, and then extend to accommodate the language needed for formal school learning. However, this does not mean a denial of the child's home language, since the child's whole identity is embedded within his or her first speech experiences. Deep emotion is embedded in home language – feelings, attitudes, expectations, fears and joys are all first expressed in the home. Denial of this is a denial of the child's whole being. And every early learning teacher knows that a classroom ethos of trust, acceptance, respect, praise and encouragement is the best environment for learning.

COMPONENTAL

develop skills and strategies to plan, monitor, reflect and transfer

Isn't it vital to concentrate on the early development of children's skills? Isn't it important to encourage young learners to think ahead and to plan? to look carefully at what they are doing? at how they are doing it? to share their ideas with the group? to remember what they did yesterday and decide how they can use that for today's activities?

EXPERIENTIAL

deal with novelty, autonomise and transfer strategies

Don't we all know that it is essential to use children's everyday experiences to bridge into new experiences? to move from the known to the unknown? to practise skills in interesting and meaningful contexts? to apply skills in new situations?

CONTEXTUAL

adapt, select and shape real-world environments

Don't we all accept that children need to adapt to the school environment that we try to make as rich as possible? Don't we encourage variety of opportunity and choice of activity? Don't we ask children how they would change things? how they would tackle the problem?

Sternberg's Triarchic Theory of Intellectual Development (extended from Wallace 2000)

Robert Sternberg (1985) has led the way in rethinking the whole concept of 'intelligence' and of the processes by which children are helped to learn effectively. He argues that although our individual genetic make-up varies with a range of strengths and weaknesses, we can all learn to use a wide range of skills and strategies for learning. These make up the components of our thinking processes: these processes in turn are made up from our mental repertoire of 'thinking tools'. We can all learn to plan and to monitor the efficiency of our planning. We can be taught how to reflect on our thinking processes in order to improve them and we can be assisted in the 'crystallisation' of 'what' we know and 'how' we learn. Then using our experiences and with mediated help, we can transfer the skills and strategies we learn to new situations and contexts. These are the key processes of metacognition: reflect, consolidate and transfer. Using our thinking and problem-solving skills, we adapt to our environment; and if we are lucky enough to be given the right opportunities, we select the environment in which we want to function. Possibly, the highest form of human endeavour is shown when we have the confidence and motivation to shape the environment around us: we become the 'movers' and the 'shakers' of the world we live in.

Think about your learning experiences:

- Which teachers do you remember with love? What characteristics did they have? How did they treat you?

- What did you learn from them? What did you learn about yourself? Can you remember the content of their lessons? Why? Why not?

- Have they influenced your style of teaching? What is the main message you have absorbed through their influence?

- How did you manage to fit the 'jigsaw pieces' of your learning together? Did you receive any help with this? Do you still retain fragments of unrelated bits and pieces of knowledge?

- What in real life has been your best learning experience? Why?

- Which are the most important skills that young children should learn?

Considering the broad teaching principles that underpin TASC

We have said earlier that outstanding teachers are 'gifted' in understanding and empathy: they use their high level of emotional intelligence to diagnose the needs of the individuals in their classrooms. Too often in this increasingly technicist society, teachers have been denied the right to use their emotional intelligence, creativity and teaching artistry in the process of professional decision-making. With the increasing emphasis on measurement of 'standards', many teachers feel that they have been relegated to the status of a classroom technician. Perhaps we should state here that no teacher denies the need for a broad curriculum framework, but the framework that emerged has been more like a straitjacket than a guide.

In early years classrooms, however, teachers have been more able to retain their autonomy and professionalism: hence the teaching principles of TASC will come as no surprise. It is important to stress again that TASC teaching principles are based on worldwide research of how children best learn and how teachers should best teach: these principles are rigorous and demand high-quality classroom practice.

The spiral diagram overleaf summarises the key teaching methodology.

Use the spiral diagram to reflect on your teaching methodology.

Reflect on the Teaching Strategies you use in the Classroom

Do you use as many real-life examples as is possible?

Do you consciously introduce thinking and problem-solving language in every activity?

Do you tell the children which skill they are practising and why the skill is important?

Do you model your own thinking 'out loud' and give names to the thinking skills you use?

Do you provide initial scaffolding such as writing frames but withdraw them as soon as the learner demonstrates confidence and competence?

Do you use children's errors as key and positive learning points?

Do you teach using a problem-solving model that you share with the learners?

Do you always give feedback to build positive self-image, motivation and independence?

Now compare your reflective audit of your teaching methodology with the essential teaching principles of TASC.

Do you deliberately work on developing a caring and sharing classroom ethos?

Do you promote cooperative and social learning as often as possible?

Do you plan activities for children to use their own initiative to solve problems?

Do you teach children the strategies of evaluating their own work?

The TASC basic teaching principles

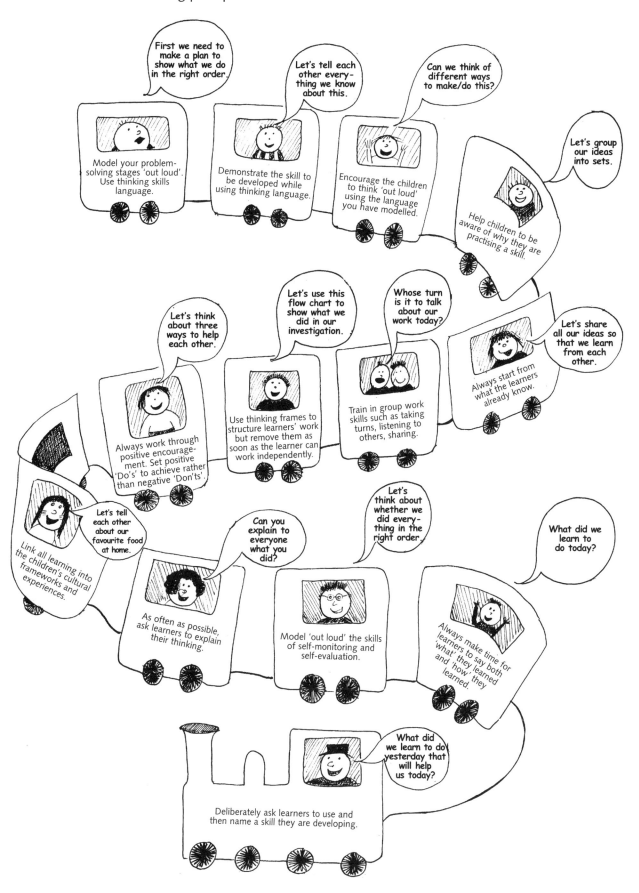

Putting the TASC problem-solving model and the teaching principles together in a menu of strategies for classroom use

Every teacher has a wide repertoire of classroom skills and strategies that are used flexibly for different purposes. Working in a problem-solving and thinking skills way doesn't mean that we should never teach from the front, organise purposeful learning by rote, practise specific skills in literacy or numeracy, or demonstrate and tell. However, when all teachers in a school are teaching in a shared problem-solving and thinking skills way, the children are receiving a coherent model and this helps them to consolidate their skills of learning how to learn.

Santa is fantastic because
he has a smiley face and
has some reindeer. And is jolly
fat. And he is jolly busy.

Hes always marvelous.
santa is always clever
Hes always fun.
santa is always kind.

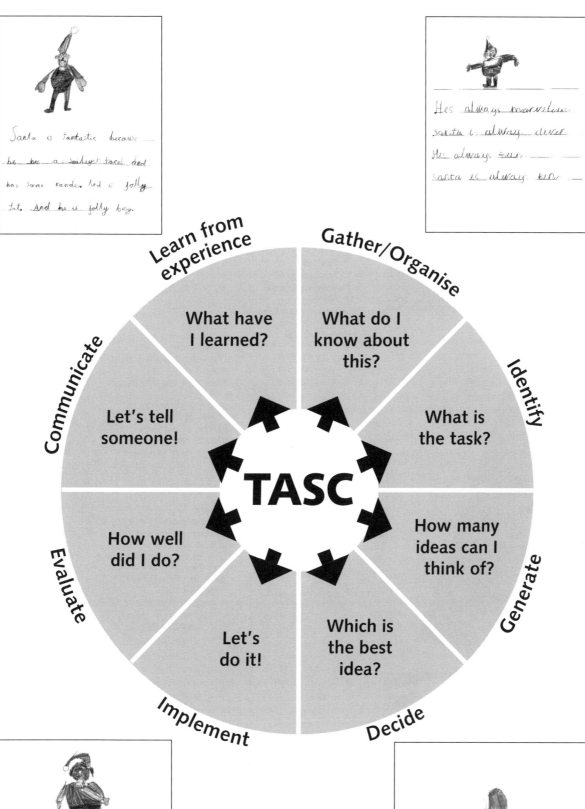

Learn from experience — **What have I learned?**

Gather/Organise — **What do I know about this?**

Communicate — **Let's tell someone!**

Identify — **What is the task?**

TASC

Evaluate — **How well did I do?**

Generate — **How many ideas can I think of?**

Implement — **Let's do it!**

Decide — **Which is the best idea?**

Santa is really brilliant
because he brings us lots
of presents. And he is jolly.
And thoughtful and
really nice.

REFLECT

Refer to the TASC Problem-solving Wheel below. Use it to reflect on the range of teaching and learning strategies you use.

The TASC problem-

✕

- Develops metacognition
- Establishes climate of learning for growth
- Gives opportunity to transfer skills and knowledge
- Crystallises what has been learned
- Gives recognition to skills learned
- Builds autonomy in learning
- Develops self-confidence and self-esteem

✕

- Develops a real purpose for task
- Encourages self-confidence
- Develops personal strengths
- Develops a repertoire of skills
- Encourages social interaction

○

- Reflect on the whole thinking process
- Compare with previous performance
- Look for uses in other lessons
- State what has been learned
- Name the skills used

○

- Create a 'real' audience
- Develop a sharing classroom
- Make real use of learners' work
- Celebrate strengths of multiple intelligences
- Make use of different learning styles
- Encourage communication

Learn from experience

What have I learned?

Communicate

Let's tell someone!

How well did I do?

TA

Evaluate

Let's do it!

✕

Start

- Builds the climate for learning how to learn
- Encourages self-assessment
- Discourages 'right first time' thinking
- Accepts mistakes as part of learning

Miss a go

Try again

Back to start

Home

○

- Check with learners if the goal was achieved
- Refer back to original idea and planning
- Think about ways to improve next time
- Give opportunity to improve
- Discuss how the group cooperated

Implement

○

- Use a variety of activities
- Teach a variety of recording skills
- Develop a range of skills for finding out
- Demonstrate new procedures

✕

- Develops multiple intelligences
- Promotes a variety of learning styles
- Encourages creativity
- Discourages 'one right way' thinking
- Promotes differentiation

solving wheel

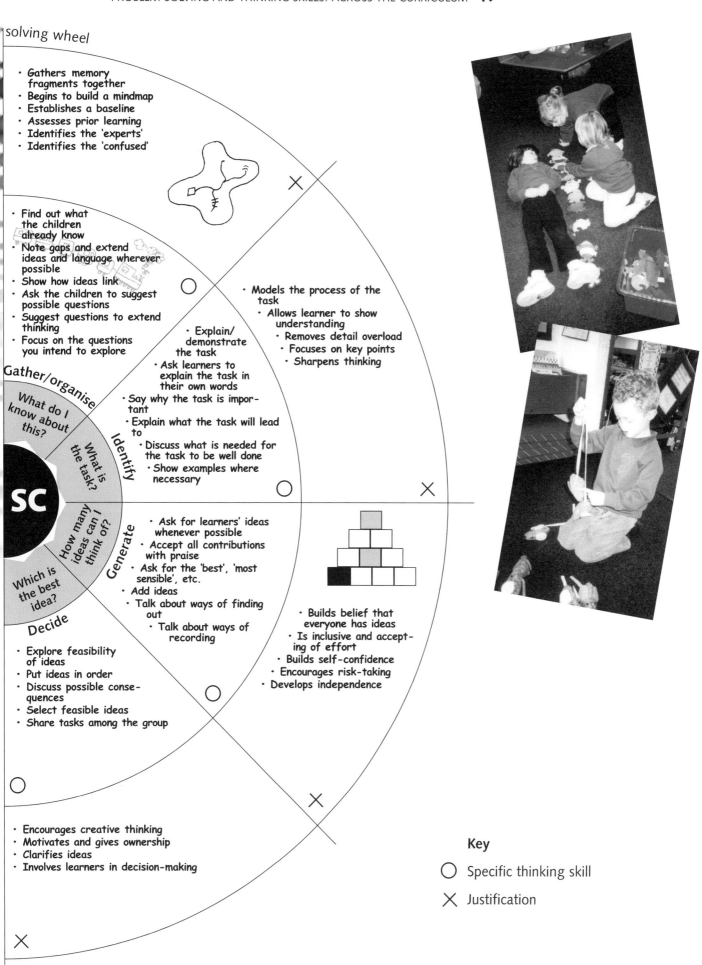

- Gathers memory fragments together
- Begins to build a mindmap
- Establishes a baseline
- Assesses prior learning
- Identifies the 'experts'
- Identifies the 'confused'

- Find out what the children already know
- Note gaps and extend ideas and language wherever possible
- Show how ideas link
- Ask the children to suggest possible questions
- Suggest questions to extend thinking
- Focus on the questions you intend to explore

- Models the process of the task
- Allows learner to show understanding
- Removes detail overload
- Focuses on key points
- Sharpens thinking

- Explain/demonstrate the task
- Ask learners to explain the task in their own words
- Say why the task is important
- Explain what the task will lead to
- Discuss what is needed for the task to be well done
- Show examples where necessary

Gather/organise
What do I know about this?

SC

What is the task?

Identify

How many ideas can I think of?

Generate

Which is the best idea?

Decide

- Ask for learners' ideas whenever possible
- Accept all contributions with praise
- Ask for the 'best', 'most sensible', etc.
- Add ideas
- Talk about ways of finding out
- Talk about ways of recording

- Builds belief that everyone has ideas
- Is inclusive and accepting of effort
- Builds self-confidence
- Encourages risk-taking
- Develops independence

- Explore feasibility of ideas
- Put ideas in order
- Discuss possible consequences
- Select feasible ideas
- Share tasks among the group

- Encourages creative thinking
- Motivates and gives ownership
- Clarifies ideas
- Involves learners in decision-making

Key

○ Specific thinking skill

✕ Justification

While all the stages of the TASC Problem-solving Wheel are important, there are four critical stages:

- **Gather and organise** This stage is important because all learners gather fragments of information but often these fragments are not linked into a whole or even partial picture. Learners need to bring what they already know into their working memory ready for 'thinking, repair, extension and action'. This process is, obviously, also an excellent tool for assessing prior learning. Importantly, learners receive the message that they do have valuable knowledge and can contribute their ideas to the learning process: the whole gathering of 'what we already know' carries the message of 'inclusion'.

- **Identify** Many learners, especially young ones, lose sight of the task they are undertaking, so it is important to encourage all learners to rephrase the task in their own words. This also helps with the evaluation stage because the learners clearly know what the purpose of the task was from the outset.

- **Evaluate** While early years teachers work through praise and encouragement of all children's efforts, even very young children can begin to learn the skills of evaluating their work with the purpose of making it even better next time.

- **Learn from experience** This stage is vital if learners are to get the message that they are growing and developing. All learners need to have the sense of progress and so they need to say to themselves 'This is what I can *do*'. Then the skills that are learned need to be called on across a wide range of activities with the teacher using the appropriate problem-solving and thinking skills language.

Developing Tools for Effective Thinking which feed into the TASC Problem-solving Wheel

In developing TASC, learners and teachers identified the Tools for Effective Thinking that they used most often in the early stages of building the children's repertoire of thinking skills. These core skills are examined below.

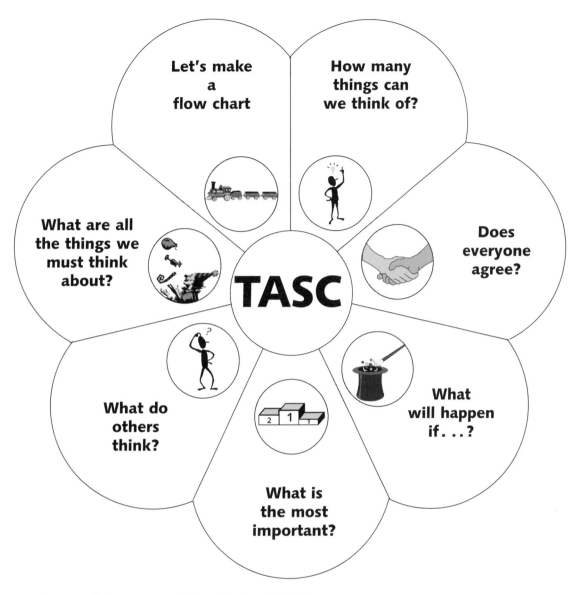

A selection of the core Tools for Effective Thinking

Modelling a 'think-tank'

- How many things can we think of?
- How many ways can we do this?

Thinking of more than one idea lies at the root of creative thinking and learners who see the unusual way or have the unusual idea need to be supported and encouraged. It is also important that children learn that their unusual ideas are acceptable so that they gain confidence in expressing things that are 'different' from the norm.

Looking at both sides of an idea

- Does everyone agree?
- Who has a different idea?

Young children tend to be very egocentric and one of the main concerns of early years educators is the development of social and sharing skills: the ability to listen to others and to see another point of view. In any learning and life situation, the ability to step into someone else's shoes is an essential skill.

What will happen if?

- What would happen if we change the end of the story?
- What would happen if we turn it upside down?

This is the tool for developing imagination and invention: young learners generally want to please their teachers and doing something 'the right way' or 'teacher's way' can inhibit their own exploration. Although some skills need to be taught for ease of working efficiently, modelling that it is OK to change things is also vitally important. Also thinking about the consequences of any action is an important thinking tool that children need to develop.

Looking all round an idea

- What are all the things we must think about before we do this?
- Have we thought of everything we need?

Taking all factors into account in any situation is also an effective learning tool. Many children leap into action without first exploring the whole idea: they impulsively launch into something when 'Let's think all about this first' is an appropriate thinking tactic to acquire.

Prioritising

- What is the most important thing to remember?
- What is the first thing we must do?

Efficient learning happens when children plan a course of action, or attend to the important things first. Often, learners waste time or work inefficiently because they haven't established any kind of order for doing something or haven't got a clear idea of what the task entails.

What do other people think?

- What would our parents say about this?

- Who can we ask to help us to do this?

Few people learn in isolation and it is important that children learn that they can consult others for help and information: in addition, they need to learn how to consult other sources of information – from people to texts.

How do the ideas link?

- Let's make a flow chart

- Let's make a star chart

Every learner learns by making links with previous knowledge and by extending these linkages into some form of mindmap. This allows learners to piece the bits and pieces together into a coherent whole, then information and ideas are easier to remember and recall.

Extending children's language for thinking

Children need to develop a language for thinking that becomes part of their natural repertoire. The best way to accomplish this is by the teacher modelling the language as he or she teaches and interacts with pupils. The following mindmap suggests a repertoire of essential language that should flow through every lesson.

COMMENT

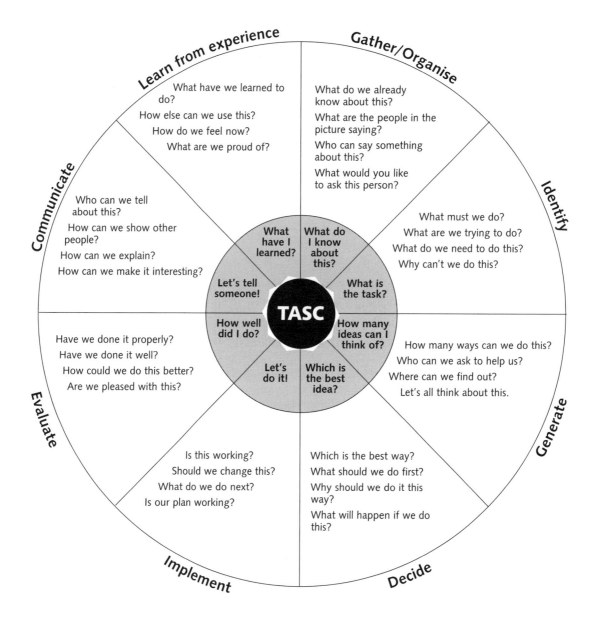

Questions to develop children's language for thinking in the TASC problem-solving model

Conclusion

There is a universal request from all sections in the adult world that schools should train children to be thinkers and problem-solvers. Without doubt the school phases using an approach nearest to a problem-solving paradigm are the Foundation Phase and Key Stage 1: it is here that teachers are most concerned with laying the basic skills of learning how to learn and learning how to think. In these early years classrooms, teachers are working to develop physical, emotional, social and cognitive skills in a holistic, integrated way.

Teachers know that young children must relate their learning to real-life experiences; that they must strengthen and use imagination and creativity; that they must develop positive self-esteem and confidence. Moreover, early years teachers know that developing problem-solving and thinking skills must be an integral way of working across all activities. For learners to become active lifelong thinkers, however, all other phases of education must take lessons from the early years classrooms. While the context of learning becomes more complex and subject based, the teaching approach should retain the holistic and integrated approach of the early years, in that learners are helped to transfer skills across the curriculum and to see the relevance of their subject knowledge to life. Attention must always be paid to the learner's self-concept and social development, not only for the benefit of the individual but also for the ultimate benefit to society.

We all learn best when we:

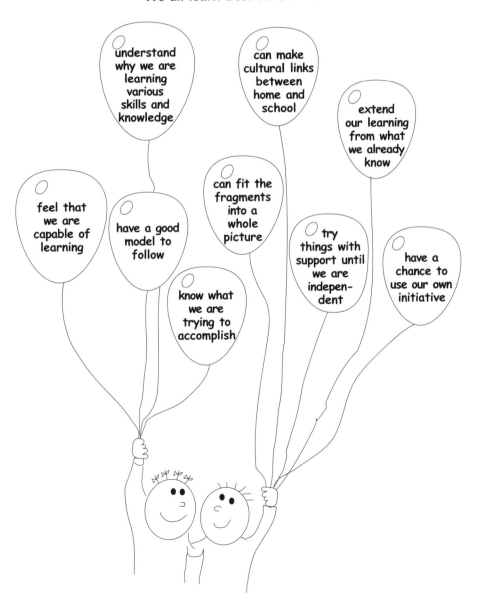

Developing learners' problem-solving and thinking skills is the greatest gift that we can give to children; and it is the greatest gift that we can give to society. The development of a humanising and empowering curriculum within a school ethos of caring and striving for excellence is surely empowering for both learners and teachers.

Examples showing the use of the TASC problem-solving model in early years classrooms (Reception and Key Stage 1)

Working across the Curriculum

The following pages (pp. 27–41) outline a series of flow-charts which show examples of classroom projects which have used the TASC model as a base for developing learning experiences for young children.

Obviously many of the flow charts that show the children's responses were recorded by the class teachers since much of the children's work was oral. Nevertheless, we can see clearly that the teachers guided the *processes* of the children's thinking throughout their oral work, leading into appropriate activities that were carried out by the young learners. Also, teachers were accepting what the children said but extending the children's language whenever it was necessary.

It is important to note that all the teachers used the TASC problem-solving wheel flexibly: selecting sections that were appropriate to the particular project they were developing, combining several sections into one extended activity, and, importantly, adapting the number of activities according to the timescale they were working to. However, over the duration of a half-term, the children can experience all stages of the problem-solving wheel, building and reinforcing the processes outlined within the wheel several times. Over a year, the children gain greater confidence and independence and begin to make their own choices about which thinking strategy they will use.

It is fascinating to see the obvious development of young learners' skills from their Reception year to Year 2, indicating very powerfully the important role of the early years teachers and their artistry in creative teaching.

My TASC problem-solving wheel

Our Teddy Bears Picnic (Reception)
Emma Jacklin and Helen Tansey
Little Gonerby CE Infant School (Lincs)

Medium-term planning

Knowledge and Understanding of the World

- to observe, find out and identify features in the place they live and in the natural world
- to select suitable materials, to assemble and join materials
- to use collage materials, to paint appropriately
- to discuss appropriate behaviour

What will happen if we store our food...?

in the fridge? ✓
It will keep cold.

in the bed?
It will get fluff on it.

in a lunch box? ✓
It will keep fresh.

in the bin?
It will be dirty.

in the cupboard? ✓
It will keep clean and tidy.

in the freezer?
It will get hard and frozen.

in the garden?
It will get wet and squashy.

on the bookshelf?
It will get dusty.

on the table?
The dog will eat it.

in the wash basket?
It will get dirty and wet.

Key: Best place ✓

Learn from experience

What I learn

Communicate

Let's tell someone!

Let's do

Evaluate

How well did I do?

Implement

Question Where is the best place to store sandwiches?

in the freezer – so that it keeps hard and frozen

in packets – so air doesn't get in

in silver foil – because it keeps fresh

in a fruit bowl – so bananas don't fall out

Let's think of all the places where food is stored

in a fridge – because it is cold

in a cupboard – so it keeps it all together

in a rack – because it has a lot of shelves

at Safeways – because there are lots of shelves

at the butchers – because there are big freezers

Key: Best place ~~~~

You are invited
to a
Picnic

On: _____

At: _____

Time: _____

_____

_____

_____

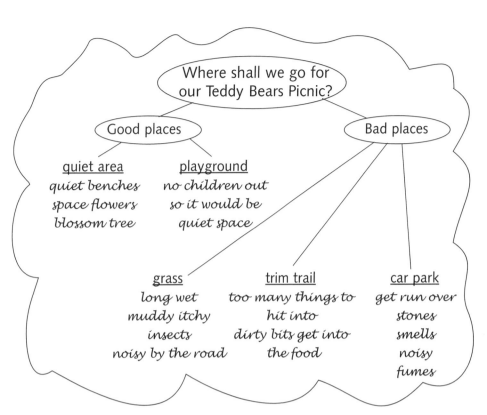

Where shall we go for
our Teddy Bears Picnic?

Good places

Bad places

<u>quiet area</u>
quiet benches
space flowers
blossom tree

<u>playground</u>
no children out
so it would be
quiet space

<u>grass</u>
long wet
muddy itchy
insects
noisy by the road

<u>trim trail</u>
too many things to
hit into
dirty bits get into
the food

<u>car park</u>
get run over
stones
smells
noisy
fumes

er/Organise

t do I
about
is?

Identify

What is
the task?

How many
ideas can I
think of?

ch is
best
ea?

Generate

Decide

What shall we eat on
our Teddy Bears' Picnic?

<u>sandwiches</u>   ice cream X   strawberries X
chocolate sauce X   <u>biscuits</u>   chocolate bar X
<u>crisps</u>   <u>sweets</u>   <u>small cakes</u>   big party cake X
yoghurt X   <u>fruit</u>   tomatoes X   <u>ham</u>
vegetables X   <u>cheese</u>

Key: Sensible ~~~~~   Not sensible X

snow

ice poles   water   rain

wind   snowballs   fog

sky   puddles

Weather

Can we
group the things
that freeze?

Food

ice cream

sausages   ice cubes

chips   strawberries   lollies

fish fingers

snow

weather

snowballs

wind

fog

chips

sky

rain

ice cubes

How
many
things
do we
know that
freeze?

snow

ice poles

sausages

ice cream

lollies

water

fish fingers

strawberries

puddles

Our Teddy Bears Picnic (Reception)

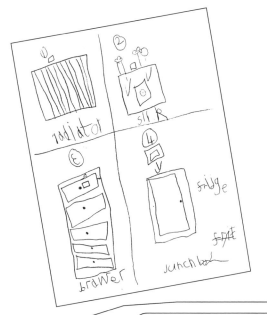

Our Investigation

What have we learned?

the sandwich in a lunch box in the fridge
soft   clean   good to eat   tasty
the sandwich in the drawer
one side is hard   the edges of the cheese are hard
the middle of the cheese is soft
the sandwich by the sink
got paint on it   wet   bread is hard   cheese is hard
the sandwich on the radiator
breaks easily   rock hard
cheese is stuck to the bread

What have we learned . . .

about storing food?
Put it in a clean fridge.
Don't put it on the
radiator.
Keep germs and dirt
away.

about freezing?
Water goes into ice.
Water gets colder.

about melting?
Ice gets warm and
melts into water.

about picnics?
It is good fun.
It's very exciting.
I like them.
You must choose a
nice place.

about investigations?
Look carefully.
Look every day.

about cooking?
You must do it in the
right order.
It is very tasty.
The chocolate is yummy.

about choosing food?
You must be sensible.
You must be clean and tidy.

Learn from experience

Communicate

What I learn

Let's tell
someone!

How well
did I do?

Evaluate

Implement

Can we draw pictures

Our Picnic — What must we do?

zzzzzzzzzzzzzzzzzz
Watch out
for wasps!

Don't forget
the Teddies!

Pick up all the
bits of paper.

Go to the
toilet before
we go

Walk in twos.

Play
games.

Don't run! You
might fall over.

Sing 'Teddy
Bears Picnic'.

Have a
nice
time.

Our Investigation

What will happen if we put our sandwich . . .

on the radiator?
It will get hot and burn.
It will fall down the back.
Flies will get on it.
The bread will change colour.
It will melt.
It will go hard. ✔ *(very)*

in the drawer?
It will get squashed.
It will get dirty. ✔
It will get lost.
It will get a sticker on it. ✔
It will get hard and stale. ✔

by the sink?
It will get wet. ✔
It will get squashed. ✔
It will get paint on it. ✔
It will get soapy. ✔

in the fridge in a lunch box?
It will get cold.
It will stay nice and fresh. ✔
It will go soggy.

Key:
What did happen? ✔

...er/Organise

...t do I
...about
...is?

What is
the task?

Identify

How many
ideas can I
think of?

Generate

...ch is
...best
...ea?

Decide

about water freezing?

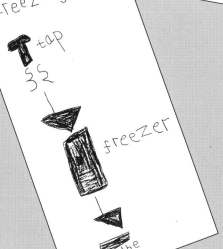

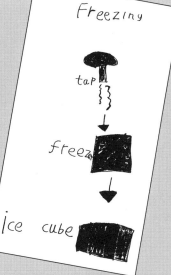

Which is the right order?

Which is the right order?

Then we put in _____ 3 rice crispies.

We melted it on _____ hot water. 2

We put the _____ 4 mixture into cases.

We put the chocolate _____ in a bowl. 1

Our Hospital Visit (Yr 1)
Marguerite Tibbett and Terry Beese
Little Gonerby CE Infant School (Lincs)

Medium-term planning
(Not all the lesson development is shown in the flowchart)

<u>English</u>
Write an account; Discuss what we found out; Answer questions; Share ideas and experiences; Write 'thank you' letters; Sequence events (POS 1.3abc, 2.1 fjl, 2.2abc, 3.1abcd, 3.3ac)

<u>History</u>
Comparison of hospitals today with hospitals 100 years ago (POS 1a, 1b)

<u>Geography</u>
Jobs in the hospital: nurses, doctors, X-ray departments, porters, receptionists, ambulance crew etc; Simple map of the journey to the hospital; Road safety (POS 1bd, 2ac, 3a)

<u>ICT</u>
Word Processing; Photographs (POS 1b, 2a, 3a)

Hospital Visit Year 1

<u>Art</u>
Painting and drawing a visit; Prioritising (POS 1a)

<u>Maths</u>
Flowchart; Sequencing; Block graph (POS 2.1g, 2.5ab)

<u>Science</u>
Investigate life processes: skeleton, bones, fractures, neck brace, body weight, blood pressure, heart beat (POS 1.2abfgl, 2.2d, 3.1d 2ab)

Learn from experience

Communicate

What did I learn?

Let's tell someone!

How well did I do?

Evaluate

Let do

Implement

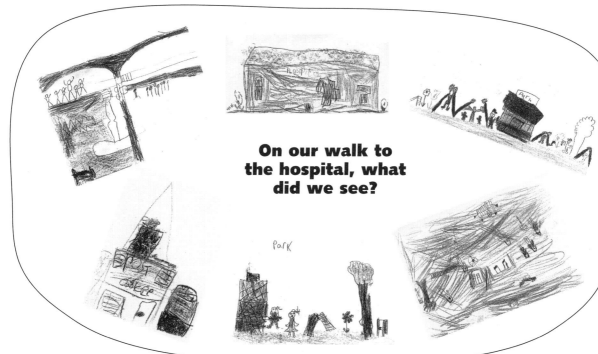

On our walk to the hospital, what did we see?

Park

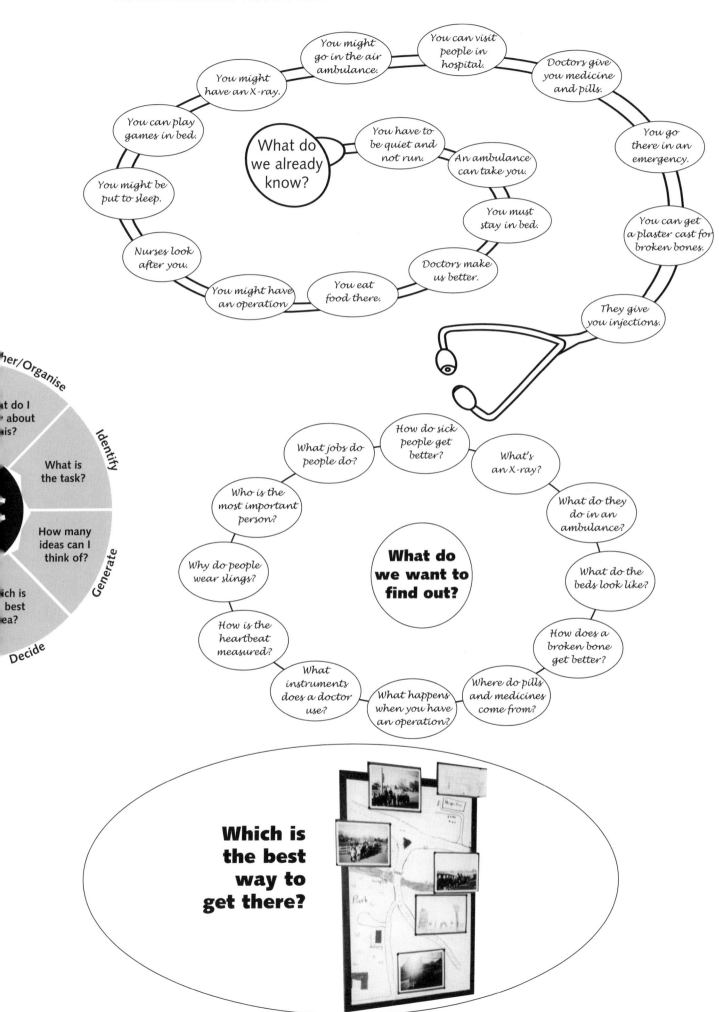

What do we already know?

You might go in the air ambulance.

You can visit people in hospital.

Doctors give you medicine and pills.

You might have an X-ray.

You can play games in bed.

You have to be quiet and not run.

An ambulance can take you.

You go there in an emergency.

You might be put to sleep.

You must stay in bed.

You can get a plaster cast for broken bones.

Nurses look after you.

You might have an operation

You eat food there.

Doctors make us better.

They give you injections.

her/Organise

at do I about is?

What is the task?

Identify

How many ideas can I think of?

Generate

ich is best ea?

Decide

What do we want to find out?

How do sick people get better?

What jobs do people do?

What's an X-ray?

Who is the most important person?

What do they do in an ambulance?

Why do people wear slings?

What do the beds look like?

How is the heartbeat measured?

How does a broken bone get better?

What instruments does a doctor use?

What happens when you have an operation?

Where do pills and medicines come from?

Which is the best way to get there?

Our Hospital Visit (Yr 1)

The scanner

The scanner is a big machine with a hole in the middle.
It takes pictures of your body from different directions.
The patient lies on the bed that goes very slowly through the hole.

The resuscitation room

We saw the heart monitoring machine and how it works.
We learned how blood pressure is taken.
We looked at an oxygen mask.
S was strapped onto a spinal board that is used to keep you still if you have injured your back.
We used a stethoscope to listen to a heartbeat.

What did we find out?

The X-ray department

An X-ray is a photograph of your bones.
A special machine takes these photographs.
You have to lie still on a bed to have these pictures taken.

The children's ward

We saw beds and cots with teddies on them.
There were toys to play with.
The children could play in the garden when they were getting better.
We had our blood pressure taken.
We all had a turn at being weighed.

The fracture clinic

We learnt what happens if you break your arm.
Mr Lewis dipped the bandage in water so it would set hard.
He used a special tool to cut the plaster off.
He showed us a skeleton that had all our bones.

Learn from experienc

Communicate

What I learn

Let's tell someone!

How well did I do?

Evaluate

Le do

Implemen

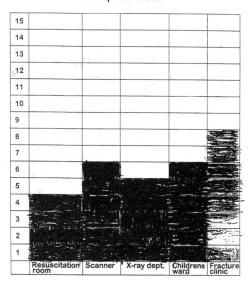

Which was the most popular department?

Hospital visit.

	Resuscitation room	Scanner	X-ray dept.	Childrens ward	Fracture clinic
15					
14					
13					
12					
11					
10					
9					
8					■
7					■
6		■			■
5		■	■		■
4	■	■	■		■
3	■	■	■		■
2	■	■	■		■
1	■	■	■		■

The most popular department was the Fracture clinic.
I liked the x ray dept best.

How could we develop our field? (Yr1/Yr2)
Natalie Bannister, Kath Lee and Shelley Tinkley
Barrowby CE Primary School (Lincs)

Medium-term planning

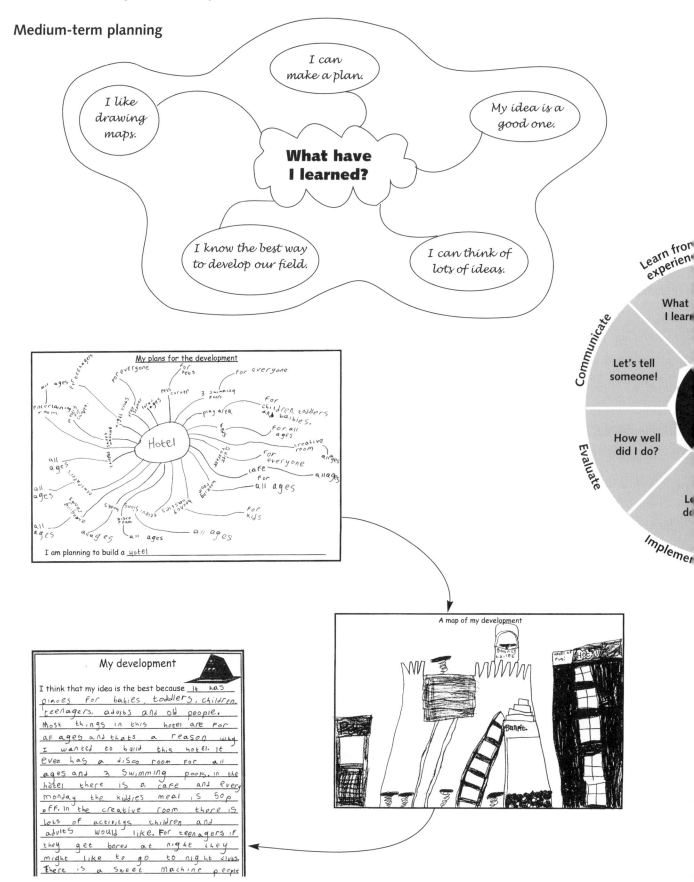

I can make a plan.

I like drawing maps.

My idea is a good one.

What have I learned?

I know the best way to develop our field.

I can think of lots of ideas.

My plans for the development

I am planning to build a Hotel

A map of my development

My development

I think that my idea is the best because It has places for babies, toddlers, children, teenagers, adults and old people. Most things in this hotel are for all ages and thats a reason why I wanted to build this hotel. It even has a disco room for all ages and 3 swimming pools, in the hotel there is a cafe and every monday the kiddies meal is 50p off. In the creative room there is lots of activitys children and adults would like. For teenagers if they get bored at night they might like to go to night clubs. There is a sweet machine people

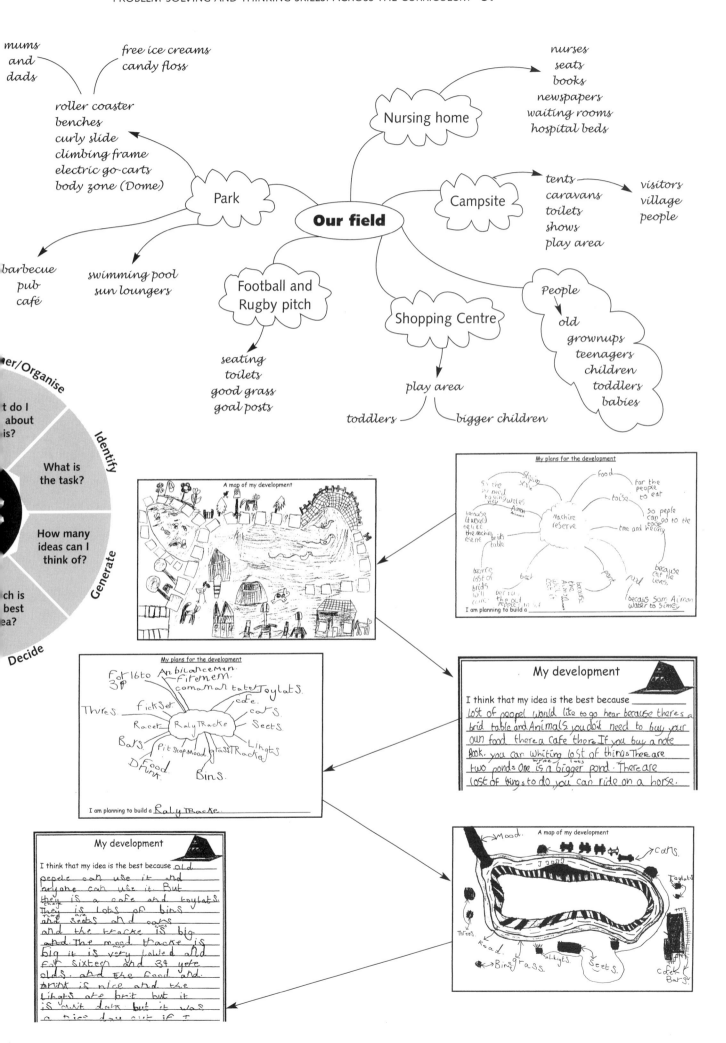

What do we know about buildings? (Rec/Yr1)
Natalie Bannister, Kath Lee and Shelley Tinkley
Barrowby CE Primary School (Lincs)

Medium-term planning

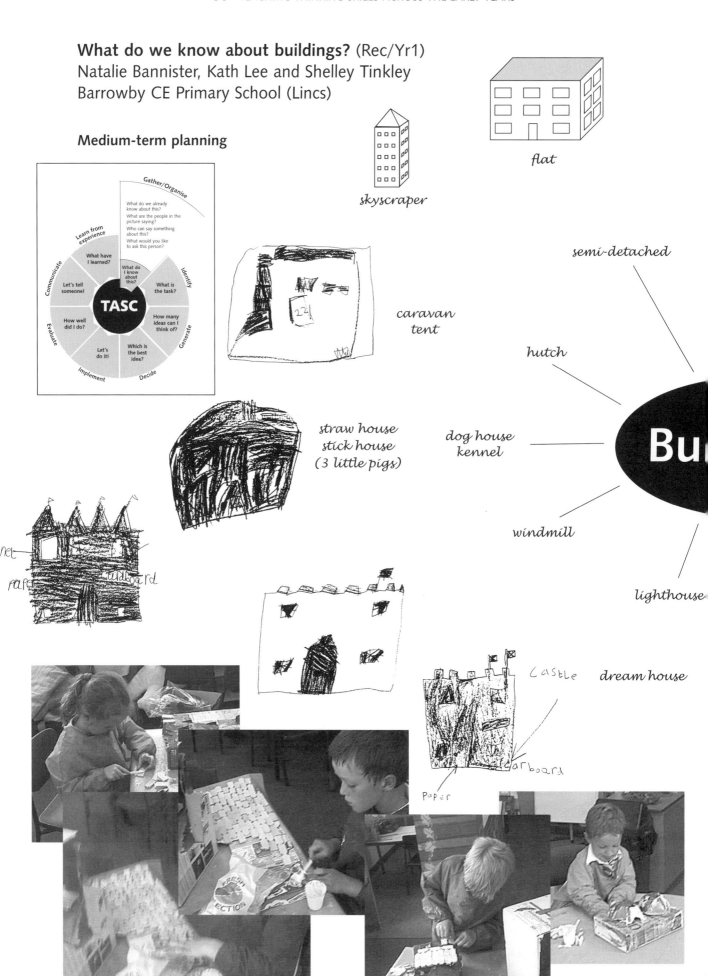

skyscraper

flat

semi-detached

caravan
tent

hutch

straw house
stick house
(3 little pigs)

dog house
kennel

Bu

windmill

lighthouse

castle

dream house

paper

cardboard

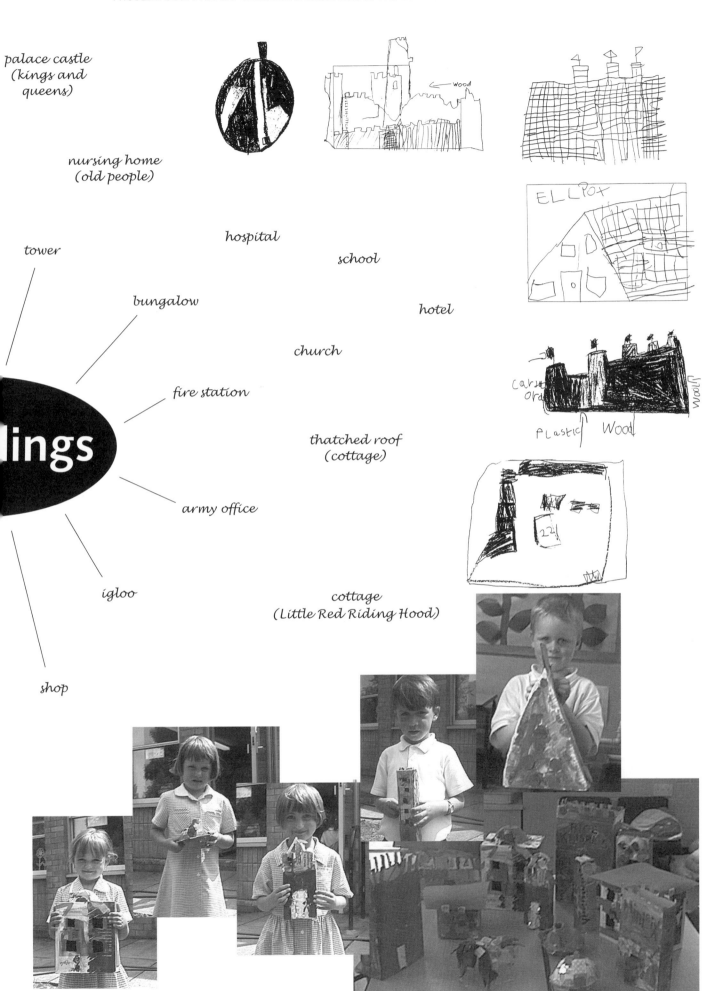

palace castle
(kings and
queens)

nursing home
(old people)

hospital

school

tower

hotel

bungalow

church

fire station

thatched roof
(cottage)

army office

igloo

cottage
(Little Red Riding Hood)

shop

ings

What do we know about castles? (Rec/Yr 1)
Natalie Bannister, Kath Lee and Shelley Tinkley
Barrowby Primary School (Lincs)

Medium-term planning

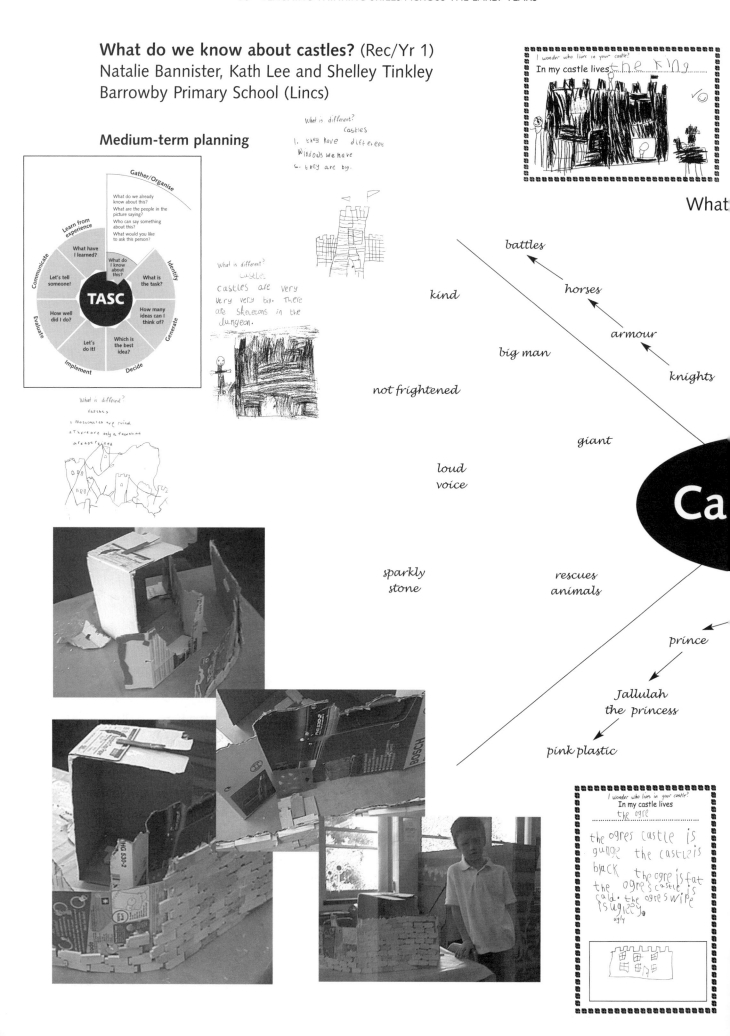

I wonder who lives in your castle?
In my castle lives the king

What is different?
Castles
1. they have different
windows we have
2. they are big.

What

battles

horses

kind

armour

big man

knights

not frightened

giant

loud
voice

Ca

sparkly
stone

rescues
animals

prince

Jallulah
the princess

pink plastic

I wonder who lives in your castle?
In my castle lives
the ogre

the ogres castle is
gunge the castle is
black the ogre is fat
the ogres castle is
cald. the ogres wipe
is ugley

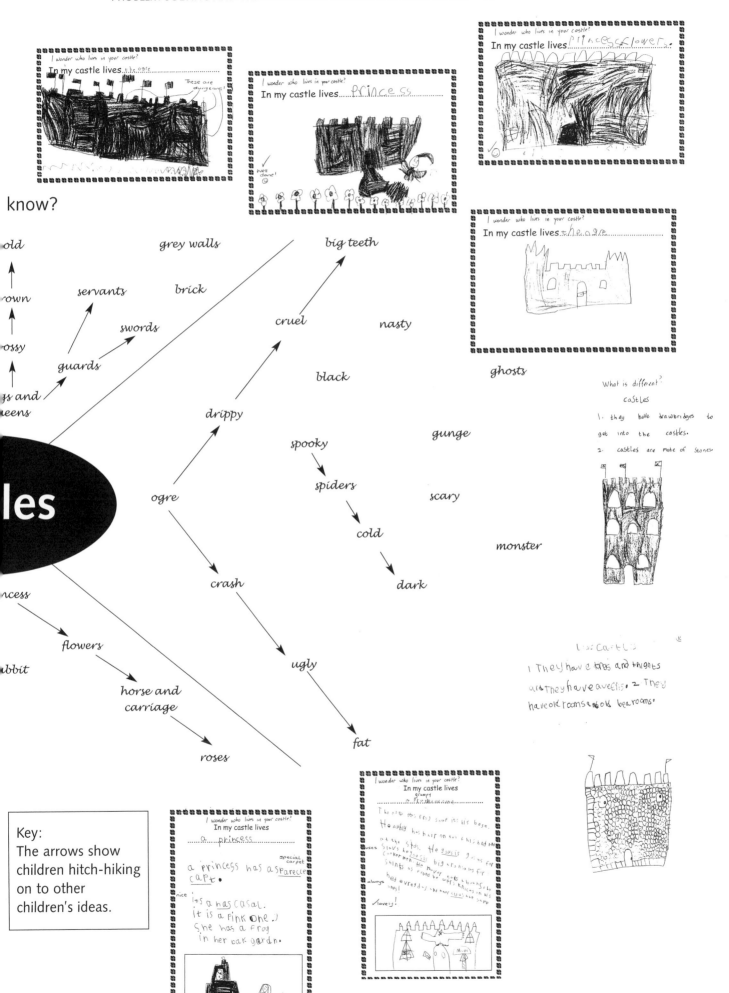

know?

old

grey walls

big teeth

rown

servants

brick

ossy

swords

cruel

nasty

guards

s and

eens

ghosts

black

drippy

gunge

spooky

ogre

spiders

scary

cold

monster

crash

dark

ncess

flowers

bbit

horse and
carriage

ugly

roses

fat

Key:
The arrows show
children hitch-hiking
on to other
children's ideas.

Some of my TASC tools for effective thinking

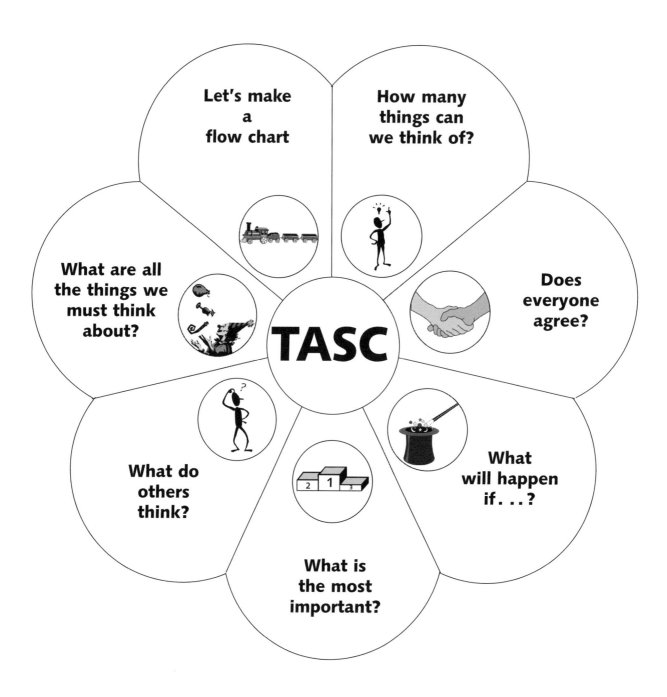

Introducing the use of the TASC Problem-solving Wheel in Reception and Key Stage 1 Literacy: Developing Children's Writing Skills

MIKE CARTER AND DOROTHY RICKARBY

The purpose of this chapter is to present a case study analysing the processes of introducing the TASC Problem-solving Wheel to a group of Reception and Key Stage 1 children. We will discuss the incremental stages of implementing new strategies in the classroom and hope that this will encourage other teachers to extend their existing classroom procedures.

 PURPOSE

Background information

 COMMENT

During the year 2000 to 2001, the headteacher (Dorothy Rickarby) and the staff of Malvern Wells CE Primary School made the decision to feature the development of thinking skills as a major target in their school development plan.

Although one of the main reasons for choosing to focus on the development of thinking skills lay in the school's desire to improve their SAT results, the staff felt that children who had experience of specific training in developing their thinking should prove to be more capable in their ability to reason, discuss and think creatively.

During the course of that year, the headteacher had tried out various approaches to the development of thinking strategies within the school, especially those linked to the development of creative writing. As part of this approach, the school had begun to use The Development of 'Thinking Through Story' materials (Dialogue Works), and to introduce the philosophical process of the creation of a community of enquiry – these processes are beginning to have an effect on children's thinking and writing.

Being open to any approaches that might add to the improvement of children's thinking within the school, the headteacher welcomed an opportunity to be involved in this case study of the use of the TASC Problem-solving Wheel with Reception and Key Stage 1 children.

At the beginning of the autumn term 2001, both the headteacher and the writer (Mike Carter) were relatively unfamiliar with the practicalities of using the TASC Problem-solving Wheel, although both were aware of its process from knowledge gained from attendance on courses and conferences. Both were somewhat apprehensive of using the total TASC Wheel with very young children, believing that the introduction of the complete process within the limited time available would be overwhelming and confusing. Once the TASC Wheel was in use, however, this belief quickly changed, for it was very apparent that even the youngest children easily assimilated the processes and became confident in their use of the TASC Problem-solving Wheel in its totality.

The TASC Problem-solving Wheel was implemented during the first half of the autumn term 2001, initially with Reception and Key Stage 1 children, and then with all Key Stage 2 children later that term. Nine lessons were devoted to the specific use of the TASC thinking processes, four with Reception and Year 1 children and five with Year 1 and Year 2 children. Lessons 4 to 9 were observed and form the basis of the observations in this chapter.

Context of the school

Malvern Wells CE Primary School is situated on the eastern side of the Malvern Hills in Worcestershire. The community forms part of the ribbon development that spreads out from the town of Malvern along the side of the hills.

The school has 97 pupils on roll. All the classes have mixed age and ability groups. There are four classes:

Key Stage 1
Reception (8) and Year 1 (8) – (total 16 pupils)
Year 1 (6) and Year 2 (15) – (total 21 pupils)

Key Stage 2
Year 3 and Year 4 (29 pupils)
Year 5 and Year 6 (31 pupils)

Reception children were new to the school at the beginning of the autumn term 2001, so had only been in school for about two weeks when the TASC thinking activities began. Of the eight Reception children admitted, all had experience of nursery school or playgroup prior to starting school.

The staffing complement for the school is head + 3.3. The head-teacher has class responsibility for Years 5 and 6 two days a week. In addition to her class responsibility, the headteacher undertook to introduce and support the teaching of thinking skills across the whole-school age range. In this way, she was able to get to know each child in the school, becoming aware of their learning potential.

Implementing the TASC Problem-solving Wheel throughout the school

As part of the school's approach to continuing professional development, the headteacher worked with each class teacher and teaching assistant during the course of a term, implementing the thinking skills programme.

The headteacher took the lead in teaching the thinking skills programme initially with the class teacher and, where appropriate, the teaching assistant observed. At times during the lesson, the class teacher and teaching assistant participated in supporting the teaching and learning, such as working with small groups or individuals with specific activities.

As the class teacher and teaching assistant became more familiar and confident with the 'new' teaching activities, they took over the lead teaching with the headteacher observing.

Following these lessons there was rigorous discussion about the quality of the teaching and its effect on the learning process, with an assessment of what the children had gained from the experience.

The overall monitoring and evaluation of teaching and learning took place during regular staff meetings where initiatives such as the implementation of the TASC Problem-solving Wheel and its effect on improving the quality of children's learning throughout the school were given serious consideration.

Preparing to implement the TASC Problem-solving Wheel

As it was the school's intention to improve the quality of the children's ability to write creatively, the content of the lessons (reproduced here) is mainly related to the generation of alternative story themes and endings. The particular strategies from the National Literacy Strategy that are featured in these lessons are shown in Table 2.3.

Although the original intention was to spread the introduction of the TASC Problem-solving Wheel over the course of a few weeks, presuming that the children would need time to become acclimatised to the different processes, it very quickly became apparent, (by the end of lesson 5) that the children were perfectly capable of assimilating the processes of the total TASC Wheel – this is visible in their responses to the various activities associated with each aspect of the TASC Wheel.

Table 2.1 compares the processes that are currently being developed in the school, across the age range. The TASC Problem-solving Wheel allows for a greater degree of refinement to be made in the development of ideas.

Table 2.1 Developing thinking skills across the curriculum

Thinking through stories (the process)	TASC Problem-solving Wheel	Community of enquiry (based on a philosophical approach)
The story is read twice.	The story is read (twice?).	Stories are told that illustrate a concept (e.g. bullying).
The children say or write their own questions about the text (what further information they want about the text).	**Gathering** information (about the story – what is known). **Generating** ideas (what we want to know about the story).	The children pose questions in response to the story.
Children agree which questions they want to discuss (e.g. by voting).	**Identifying** the purpose – arising from ideas generated or guided by the teacher.	
These questions are discussed in pairs/groups or with the whole class.	**Implementing** (carrying out the task).	Through shared discussion and negotiation, children discuss the answers they have obtained to their questions.
Teacher manages the direction the discussion can take (because of prior knowledge of the story and the outcome required).		The teacher acts as an enabler to promote discussion.
Particular skills can be featured (arising from the children's questions) that can be developed (analytical thinking).	**Communicating**, sharing information, providing explanations, refining suggestions.	
	Deciding which questions will be used (selecting the direction governed by the lesson objective). Justification of choices and actions. **Evaluating** (depending on the outcome – Has the lesson objective been fulfilled?).	
	Reflecting (Have we discovered something new?).	

Lesson planning

The broad outlines of lessons shown in Table 2.2 demonstrate the way the TASC Problem-solving Wheel was to be developed over the course of the first half of the autumn term 2001.

Table 2.2 Lesson outlines and expected outcomes (Reception and Year 1/Years 1 and 2)

Lesson	Outline	Expected outcome
1	What is thinking? Initial session to focus on thinking.	To encourage children to become reflective.
2	Use of symbols Preparing children for using the TASC Wheel.	To devise symbols to represent different thinking skills and activities.
3	**(Reception/Year 1)** *The wind blew* by Pat Hutchins[1] Using the story to promote discussion.	To begin to use the TASC Problem-solving Wheel – gathering, generating ideas and identifying the task.
4	**(Years 1 and 2)** *Can you weigh an elephant?* by Derek Farmer[2] Using the story to promote discussion and the development of alternative story themes.	To begin to use the TASC Problem-solving Wheel – gathering and generating ideas; plotting other incidents of types of TASC thinking on the Wheel as they arise in discussion (e.g. implementing and communicating).
5	**(Reception/Year 1)** 'How would you wash an elephant?' (arising out of the story *Can you weigh an elephant?* by Derek Farmer Using the story to promote discussion and the development of alternative story themes.	To begin to use the TASC Problem-solving Wheel – gathering and generating ideas; plotting other incidents of types of TASC thinking on the Wheel as they arise in discussion (e.g. implementing and communicating).
6	**(Reception/Year 1)** **Continuation of (Lesson 5) 'How would you wash an elephant?' from *Can you weigh an elephant?* by Derek Farmer** Development of alternative story themes.	To explore the use of all the elements of the TASC Problem-solving Wheel, particularly deciding, evaluating and reflecting.
7	**(Years 1 and 2)** **'Will a boat be able to float with an elephant in it?' (arising out of *Can you weigh an elephant?* by Derek Farmer** Continuation of Lesson 4 with a science bias (floating and sinking).	To have experience of all the TASC Wheel thinking strategies, especially deciding, evaluating, communicating and reflecting skills.
8 (R/Y1) **9** (Y1/Y2)	**(Reception/Year 1) and (Years 1 and 2)** **Story endings** Part of a story is read or told; the children are asked to provide a credible ending to the story.	Experience of using the complete TASC Problem-solving Wheel. Emphasis on selecting from a range of possible endings the most appropriate ending. Focus on deciding, communicating, evaluating and reflecting.

[1] Pat Hutchins (1994) *The wind blew.* London: Random House.
[2] Derek Farmer (1990) *Can you weigh an elephant?* London: Longman.

Table 2.3 How the National Literacy Strategy (text level work) featured in the TASC thinking lessons (4 to 9) (Source: Department for Education and Employment (DfEE) (1998) *National Literacy Strategy.* London: DfEE.)

Ref. (NLS)	Text level work	Visible in TASC lesson
R9	To be aware of story structures (actions, reactions, consequences) and the ways that stories are built up and concluded.	4
R13	To think about and discuss what they intend to write, ahead of writing it.	6, 8, 9
R14	To use experience of stories … and simple recounts as a basis for independent writing, e.g. re-telling, substitution, extension and through shared composition with adults.	4, 5, 6, 7
Y1.1.5	To describe story settings and incidents and relate them to own experience and that of others.	4, 5, 6
Y1.1.9	To write about events in personal experience linked to a variety of familiar incidents from stories.	8, 9
Y1.2.4	To re-tell stories, giving the main points in sequence and to notice differences between written and spoken forms in re-telling.	6, 8, 9
Y1.2.6	To identify and discuss a range of story themes…	4, 5, 6, 8, 9
Y1.2.7	To discuss reasons for, or causes of, incidents in stories.	5, 6, 7, 8, 9
Y1.2.8	To identify and discuss characters…to speculate how they might behave…	4, 5, 6, 8, 9
Y1.2.10	To identify and compare basic story elements, e.g. beginnings and endings in different stories.	8, 9
Y1.2.14	To represent outlines of story plots using e.g. captions, pictures, arrows to record main incidents in order…	6, 8, 9
Y1.3.5	To re-tell stories, to give the main points in sequence and to pick significant preferences and give reasons.	8, 9
Y1.3.8	To compare and contrast stories with a variety of settings…	8, 9
Y1.3.21	To use the language and features of non-fiction texts, e.g. labelled diagrams…	6, 7
Y2.1.4	To understand time and sequential relationships in stories, e.g. what happened when…	8, 9
Y2.1.11	To use language of time to structure a sequence of events…	8, 9
Y2.1.17	To use diagrams in instructions, e.g. drawing and labelling diagrams…	6, 7

R = Reception   Y = Year

Shaded area = overlap of age range between classes
Bold line = class age range divide (Reception and Year 1; Years 1 and 2)
Length of lessons: Reception/Year 1 – approximately 30 minutes   Years 1 and 2 – approximately 45 minutes

The lessons were spread over the course of the first half of the autumn term 2001 – usually one lesson a week with each year group.

The headteacher was the 'lead teacher' for each of the lessons shown above and is referred to in the observations as 'the teacher'.

Each lesson had additional adult support – the class teacher and teaching assistant were observing the way in which the TASC process could be developed with their class, not only for the development of creative writing, but for use across the whole curriculum range. This is part of the school's process of continuing professional development.

The writer was present as an observer in Lessons 4 to 9.

The lessons
Reception and Year 1

No of children	Lessons
8 Reception, 8 Year 1	5, 6 and 8

Lesson 5

'How would you wash an elephant?' – (arising out of the story *Can you weigh an elephant?* by Derek Farmer

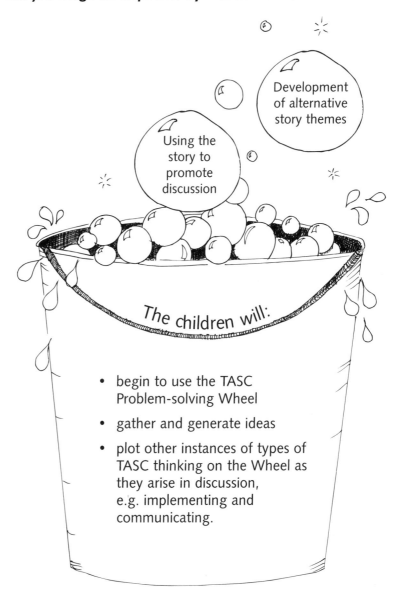

Development of alternative story themes

Using the story to promote discussion

The children will:

- begin to use the TASC Problem-solving Wheel

- gather and generate ideas

- plot other instances of types of TASC thinking on the Wheel as they arise in discussion, e.g. implementing and communicating.

The children are being introduced to some of the aspects of the TASC Problem-solving Wheel. The teacher opens a discussion about thinking and asks the children to suggest 'how we could show ourselves thinking – perhaps using symbols to show what we are doing'.

Children suggest smiley faces (one looking serious – to show concentration; another smiling with a tick over the head – to show 'we have thoughts in our brains'). These symbols are drawn on segments of paper and will be used to construct a TASC Wheel.

Gathering information

What do we know about books?

The teacher uses one of the smiley face symbols to indicate the thinking process the children are engaged in as they discuss what they know about books.

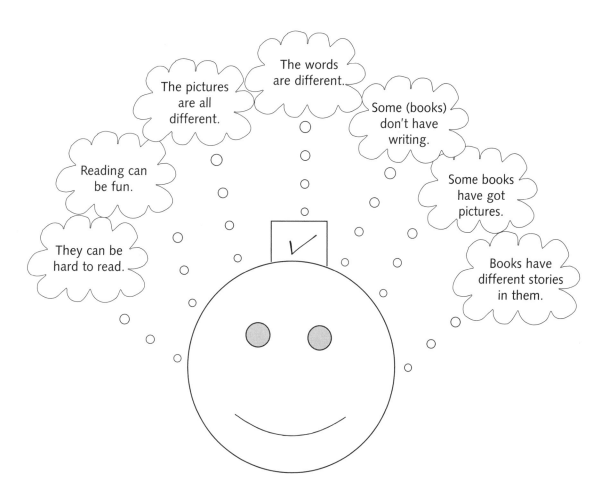

What do we know about a book before we start reading it?

The children talk about the way in which the picture on the cover provides a clue to what the story might be; older children know about titles.

What do you think this story is about?

Children provide various responses governed by what they see on the front cover – such as 'elephants', 'boats', 'people going on a boat trip', some of the older children are able to read the title.

Generating ideas

The teacher begins to read the story and pauses after reading the introduction.

She encourages the children to think of any questions they want to ask, at any time, if it will help them understand the story. As she says this she uses another segment of paper and draws lots of question marks on it indicating '**generating ideas**'.

The story features an elephant being given as a present to the Emperor of China. As the children ask questions, the teacher writes them on a whiteboard for them to see and read.

More of the story is read, with the teacher stopping at intervals to allow the children to ask any questions they wish. All questions are recorded on the white board and referred to, especially when similar questions are asked: 'I think we have got that question already – what do you think?'

At the point in the story where the elephant has a bath, a child asks 'Why does the elephant have to have a bath?' Other - children begin to provide reasons:

The teacher reminds the children that they are thinking about questions to ask and that answers are not needed at this stage.

The children find it difficult to rephrase the answers in the form of questions:

Some time is spent discussing this matter with them and practising turning statements into questions.

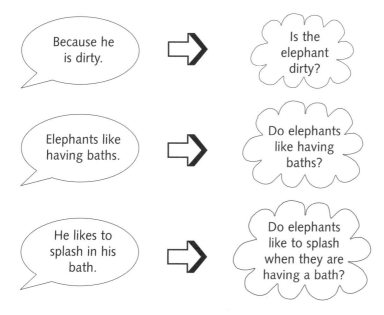

This was the first occasion on which the specific features of the TASC Wheel were introduced.

The teacher was apprehensive about whether the youngest children would be able to be fully involved with the process, so only two aspects of the Wheel were tentatively introduced: **gathering and generating**.

Lesson 6

Continuation of (Lesson 5) 'How would you wash an elephant?'
(from *Can you weigh an elephant?* by Derek Farmer)

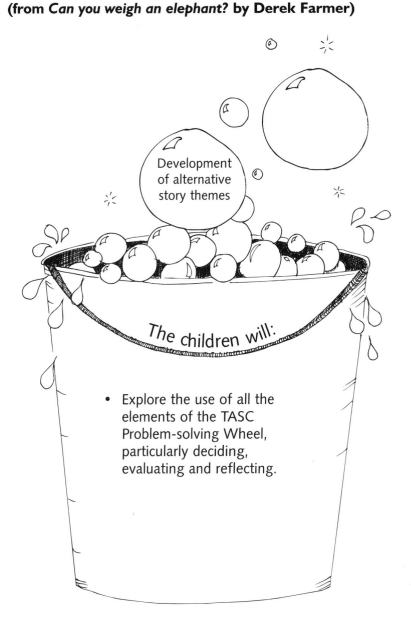

Development of alternative story themes

The children will:

- Explore the use of all the elements of the TASC Problem-solving Wheel, particularly deciding, evaluating and reflecting.

COMMENT ▶ Following the previous lesson and two lessons with children from Years 1 and 2, it became apparent that to continue introducing the TASC Problem-solving Wheel processes stage by stage would (a) take too long to implement and, more importantly, (b) was impeding children's thinking – depriving them of other, necessary stages that were important parts of the thinking process. The process needed to be viewed holistically rather than incrementally.

As a result, all future lessons, for both the younger and older children, would feature the entire thinking process as represented by the TASC Wheel.

Gathering information

The lesson opens with the teacher recalling the previous week's theme about the reasons why the elephant needed to be bathed.

Do you remember why the elephant needed to be bathed?

Identifying the task

Identify

Let's think of all the ways we could bath an elephant.

Generating ideas

Gather

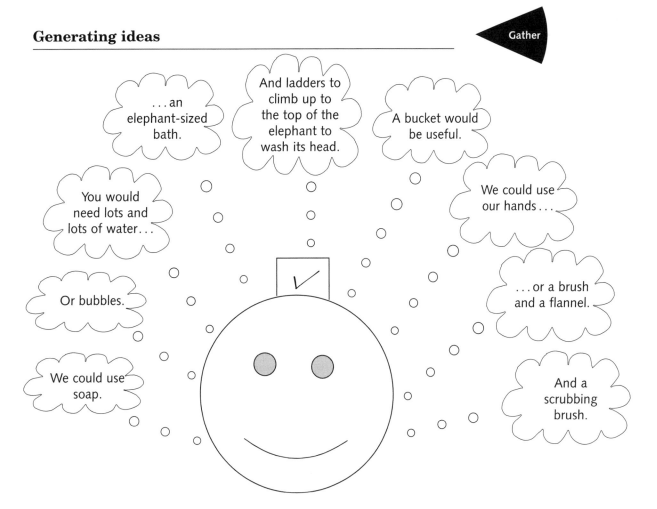

This discussion seems to capture the children's imagination and ideas come thick and fast. All are written on the whiteboard for children to read.

Decide ▶ **Deciding**

We have all these different ideas for bathing an elephant.

Now we need to **decide** *how to do this.*

Children read through the list on the whiteboard and are then asked to show by drawing and writing (if they are able to), how the elephant could be bathed. They are asked to produce a drawing that shows how the process will work and not to produce a picture (a diagram rather than a piece of art work). They are given about ten minutes to complete the process.

Implementing

The three adults in the class (teacher, class teacher and writer) ask the children to discuss their written/drawn responses and,

where necessary, scribe their comments. All children appear to appreciate the difference between 'a drawing to show an action' (a diagram) and 'a piece of art work'. No child spends much time on the drawing – all are quite voluble about what their diagrams represent.

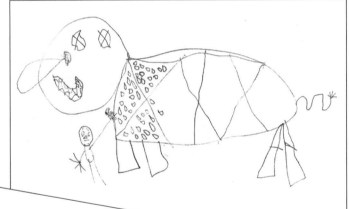

Evaluating

The teacher explains that the story could make use of any of the children's ideas, but on this occasion, only two suggestions for the elephant's bath are going to be used.

The children's written/ drawn responses are spread out on tables around the room and two children are asked to select the responses they think best relate to the story (not the picture they like best!). One chooses a diagram of an elephant being bathed in the sea (sea group), and the other chooses an elephant being bathed in a large bath (bath group).

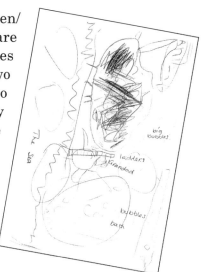

Communicating

The children are asked to group themselves (physically) into the 'sea' or 'bath' groups, but in choosing the group to be in, 'each person has to be prepared to explain their reasons for choosing the way they have done it'.

Reflecting

The teacher draws a circle with eight segments on the white-board, representing the TASC Wheel. She summarises what the children have experienced during the lesson, and as she reviews each part of the thinking process, she draws a symbol in one of the segments to illustrate the type of thinking being reviewed:

● We started off by **gathering** what we could remember of the story we started last week.

● We **identified** what we had to do today, and that was to think about the way we could bath an elephant.

● We **generated** (thought about) lots of different ways we could bath an elephant.

● After that, we **decided** on just two ways that we could bath the elephant.

● Then we **implemented** our ideas by drawing diagrams of how we thought we could bath an elephant.

● Then we **evaluated** or gave our reasons for why we thought one or other of the ways of bathing an elephant was the best way to do it.

● We **communicated** or shared our thinking about why we thought the way we did – in fact, we have done a lot of **communicating** this morning, sharing our thinking with each other.

● And now, finally, we are thinking about thinking or **reflecting** on what we have done during the lesson together. One of the children comments that she 'enjoyed thinking about thinking!', another says that she 'liked thinking about all the different ways of washing the elephant.'

The lesson demonstrated that the children were quite capable of managing all the stages of the TASC Problem-solving Wheel as a continuous process.

TASC terminology was used appropriately (as featured in bold type above) and children were not 'talked down to' but were encouraged to use the terminology themselves.

Helping children to understand what 'evaluation' means was effectively managed through the process of restricting or focusing choice and then asking them to 'take sides' to show, literally, where they stood regarding their opinion or judgement.

The children needed to be reminded that in making a choice, each needed to be prepared to give reasons for that choice.

Lesson 8

Story endings

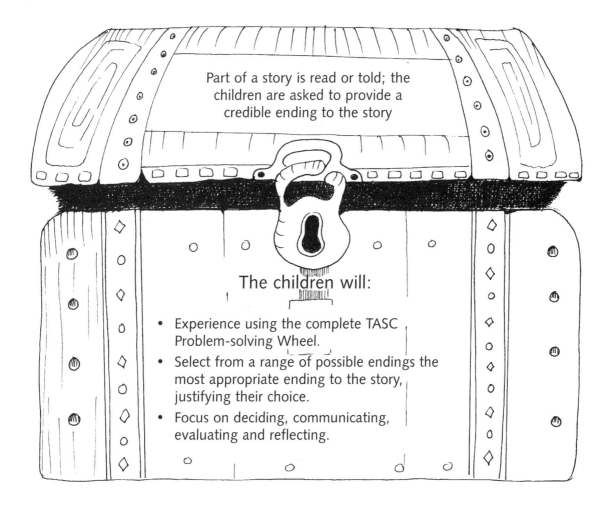

Part of a story is read or told; the children are asked to provide a credible ending to the story

The children will:

- Experience using the complete TASC Problem-solving Wheel.
- Select from a range of possible endings the most appropriate ending to the story, justifying their choice.
- Focus on deciding, communicating, evaluating and reflecting.

The session begins by reviewing the different ways of thinking that the children have experienced during the previous sessions. Reference is made by the teacher to a diagram of the TASC Wheel to illustrate the various processes.

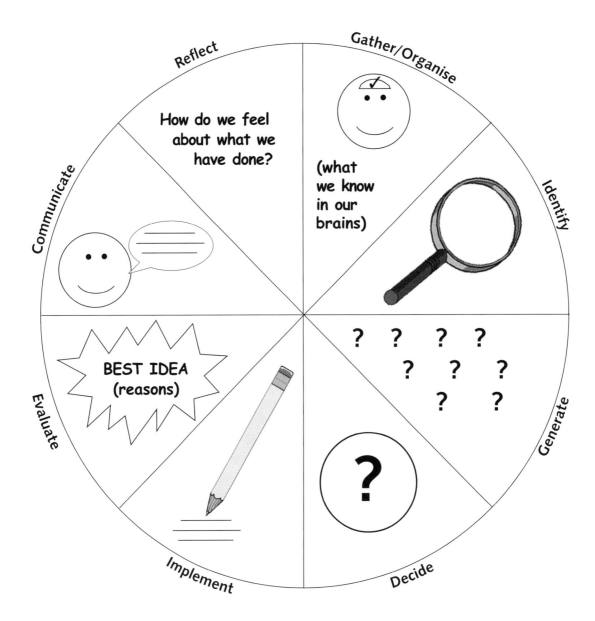

An attempt to create a set of standardised symbols to represent the types of thinking on the TASC Wheel with Y1/Y2

Gathering information

The teacher shows the children an attractively coloured box in which an object is hidden, she is going to tell them a story about the object, but first the class has to guess what the object is. The children are given a phonic clue – the object begins with the letter 'b', (a small hand bell).

The children give various responses, for example butterfly, banana, balloon, book, bulb etc. Each of their suggestions is written on the whiteboard and referred to and read back.

After several minutes, Mandy, one of the youngest children in the class, says (almost in frustration): 'Oh go on, tell us what it is! We want to know!' At which point, the teacher tinkles the bell inside the box.

Generating ideas

The teacher begins to tell a story about the bell, and then, at the crucial point in the story, says that the bell has mysteriously disappeared. What she wants the children to do is to think about what might have happened to the bell.

Many explanations are given for the bell's disappearance – all of which are recorded on the whiteboard and read back with the children.

Identifying the task

The children are asked to produce a credible explanation for the disappearance of the bell, which would relate well to the start of the story.

Implementing

The children record their explanations in writing or diagrammatic form (as they had done in Lesson 6).

Adults within the classroom discuss the children's responses with them and scribe for those children who need support with their writing.

Communicating

After ten minutes, the children are asked to share their responses. There are five main categories of response:

● Magical disappearance.

● The bell had rolled off the dressing table and under something (e.g. bed).

● A bat had flown in and taken it/knocked it out of the window.

● The bell had 'smashed'.

● The bell had been thrown into the bin by someone.

Deciding

The children are asked 'to vote' for the story ending they think most appropriate by joining one of the five groups (or categories), being prepared to provide a reason for their selection – which story ending they think most likely and that relates well to the initial part of the story.

Evaluating

These are some of the explanations given:

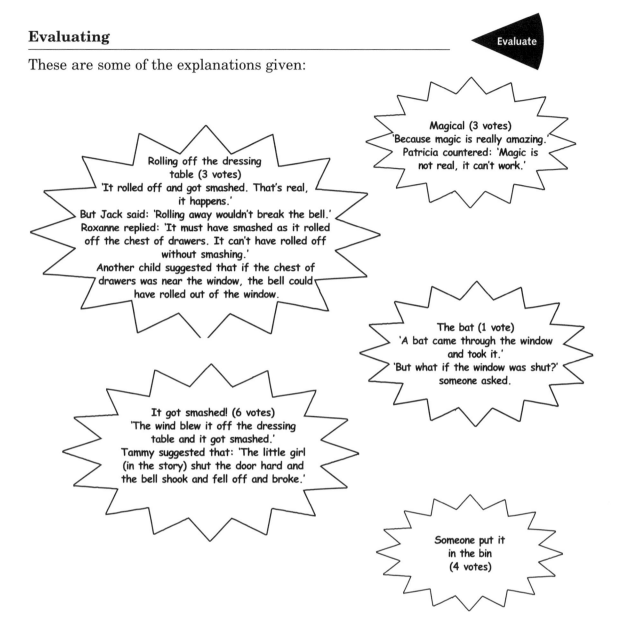

During this discussion about the probability of some of the outcomes, Roxanne indicates that she wants to change her mind and alter her vote and move to a different group (she moves from the 'binned' group to the 'smashed' group – see above).

Reflecting

The TASC process is reviewed in much the same way as was done at the end of Lesson 6. Children say they enjoy the process of voting, being able to share other people's ideas and participate in a selection process.

There is some discussion about 'changing one's mind' as Roxanne had done, showing that she had been persuaded by what other people had to say. The teacher remarks that, 'Changing your mind, or being persuaded by someone else's ideas is quite a difficult thing to do, and then to be able to admit that you have changed your mind needs a lot of courage, especially when you are prepared to say why you are doing this.'

The lesson reinforced the realisation gained from the previous week that children are able to manage the total TASC Problem-solving Wheel with confidence. Some of the most confident children were those who had only been in school for about five weeks.

The use of 'voting' as part of the **deciding** and **evaluating** aspects of thinking reinforced the understanding of what deciding is about.

Warning the children that having made a decision, they needed to be aware of their reasons for doing so in order to justify their choice, appeared to be readily understood even by the youngest child, and was a powerful part of making the process of 'reasoning' come alive.

Roxanne's decision to change her mind showed how powerful is the ability to put forward a persuasive viewpoint and again shows the value of engaging in this form of thinking activity at an early stage in a child's education. As the teacher explained, there is also a degree of maturity in being able to concede a point and perceive someone else's views.

Years 1 and 2

No of children	Lessons
6 Year 1 15 Year 2	4, 7 and 9

Lesson 4

Can you weigh an elephant? **by Derek Farmer**

Using the story to promote discussion and the development of alternative story themes

The children will:
- begin to use the TASC Problem-solving Wheel
- gather and generate ideas
- plot other instances of types of TASC thinking on the Wheel as they arise in discussion e.g. implementing and communicating.

The lesson opens with a review of what the children had considered in the previous session on thinking. The teacher explains that she is shortly going to read the children a story and that she wants the children to interrupt with questions as and when they occur to them. The title is deliberately withheld so as not to provide any clues about possible outcomes in the story.

The first page or so of *Can you weigh an elephant?* is read (some of the children appear to know the story).

Every so often, the teacher pauses and invites the children to think of questions that would provide them with more information about what is happening within and around the story (inferential comprehension).

Synopsis of story used in the lesson

The story tells of an elephant being sent as a present to an emperor in China. No one in that part of the world has seen an elephant or knows what one is. The elephant arrives in a boat, wrapped up in paper with a bow on its head ...

Generating ideas

Questions are asked by the children – these are written on a whiteboard as the children ask them.

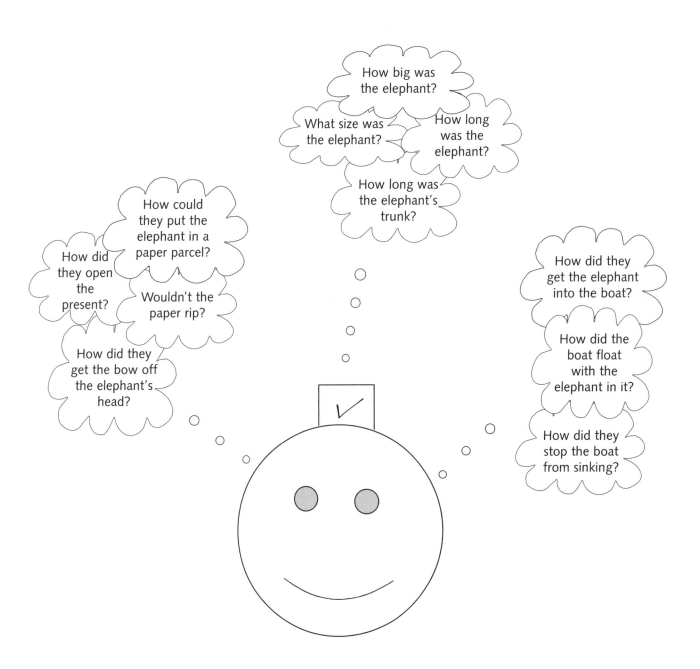

Having **generated** these questions, the children are asked which questions they wish to consider in more detail. (The children are only allowed to have one choice from the list of questions on the whiteboard.)

Most of the children are obviously intrigued by the questions:

- How did they get the elephant into the boat?

- How did the boat float with the elephant in it? (this being the most popular question indicated by the choices)

At this point, the teacher divides the class into several groups to consider the question: 'How did the boat float with the elephant in it?' (The adults in the class scribe the children's responses).

After about five minutes of discussion, the children return to a plenary session where they review the responses they had made to the question; but before they begin this process, the teacher informs them that when they tell her what they have been thinking about, she is going to use some symbols to show them the type of thinking they have been using.

The children are asked to explain what they think is meant by 'using symbols'.

Lesson 7

'Will a boat be able to float with an elephant in it?' (arising out of *Can you weigh an elephant?* by Derek Farmer)

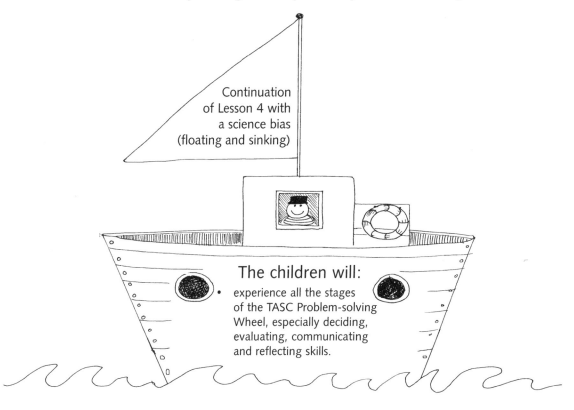

Gathering information

Recalling the activity from the previous session where the children had considered how the boat would float when carrying the elephant, there is some discussion about the concepts of 'mass and heaviness'.

Some children talk about boats being made of metal, 'so that they could carry very heavy weights (cargoes)'; others, in trying to understand the concept of producing the lightest boat to carry a heavy cargo such as an elephant, suggest boats made from grass (cf. the reed boats of Egypt and Peru).

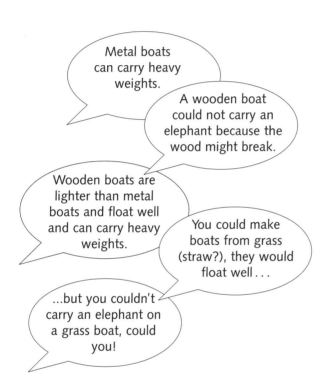

After some discussion about the concepts of floating and sinking, the class consensus favour the idea that wooden boats are more likely to float, and therefore be able to carry heavy weights, 'because wood is lighter than metal'.

Identifying the task

The teacher suggests that the children might like to consider making a model boat (at a later stage) that could carry a heavy weight in order to test some of their ideas, 'so it is important to think carefully about the design of the boat and the materials you will need for its construction'.

Generating ideas

The children are asked to consider the type of materials that can be used to make a model boat capable of carrying a heavy weight, e.g. a stone to represent the elephant.

A list of materials is made.

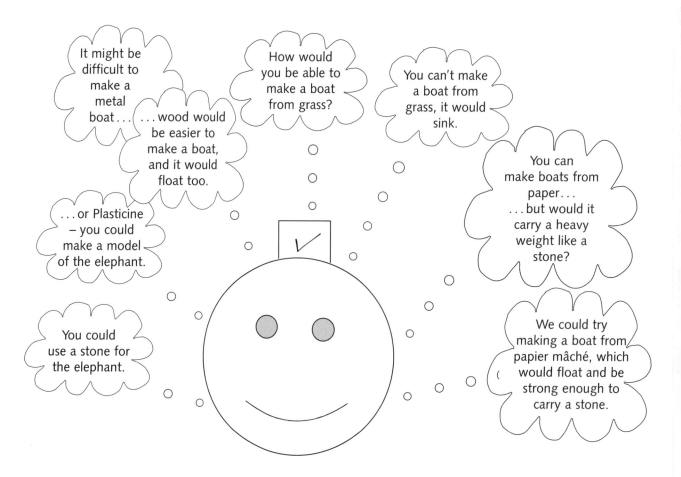

Implementing

Given the fact that the model boat is required to carry a heavy weight (a stone), the children are asked to produce a design of their boat. They are reminded to think about the materials they wish to use for the construction of the model, as this will affect the boat's size and design and capability to carry a heavy weight, such as a model elephant or a stone to represent the elephant.

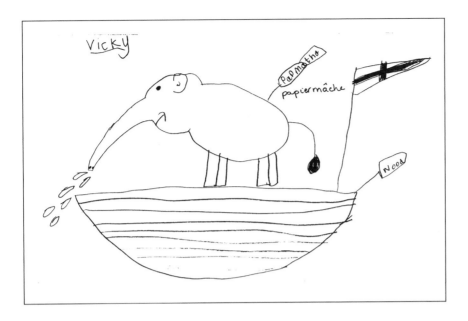

As with the younger children, the teacher stresses the importance of producing a functional, labelled drawing or diagram and not a picture of a boat.

Deciding and communicating

Decide & Communicate

Ten minutes is allowed for producing a design, at which point all the designs are spread out for the children to view and decide which design is most appropriate.

As with the younger children, the teacher reminds the children that they must be prepared to give reasons for their choice.

After some discussion about the designs and their fitness for the purpose of carrying a heavy weight, two children are chosen to make a selection.

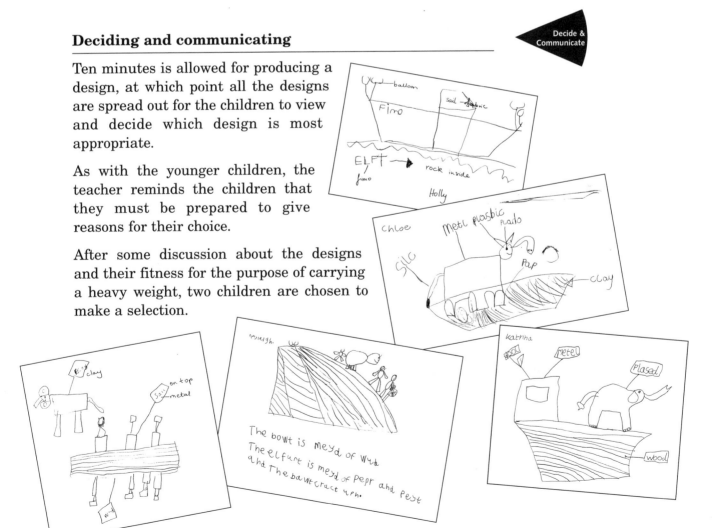

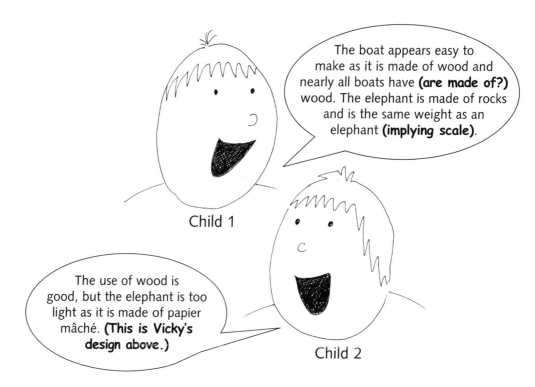

 **Learning**

At this stage in the process, the term 'Learning' is being used. On being asked what they thought they had learnt from the activity, the children appear to be providing answers that they think will 'please the teacher', such as, 'We are learning to think', or 'We have learnt to explain how we chose a design.'

The term 'Learning' is replaced by 'Reflecting', which provides greater opportunities for the children to respond to questions such as:

● What surprised us?

● Have we discovered something we didn't know about before?

● Have we noticed something about the way [a person] has worked?

COMMENT ▶

This was the first occasion when the class used the total TASC Problem-solving Wheel.

Although the scientific issues raised by the children about 'mass' and 'weight' and their relationship to 'floating and sinking' were not explored by the class on this occasion, the TASC Problem-solving Wheel is ideally suited to a scientific investigation into these issues at another time.

The following outline shows how the TASC Problem-solving Wheel could be used in such a situation:

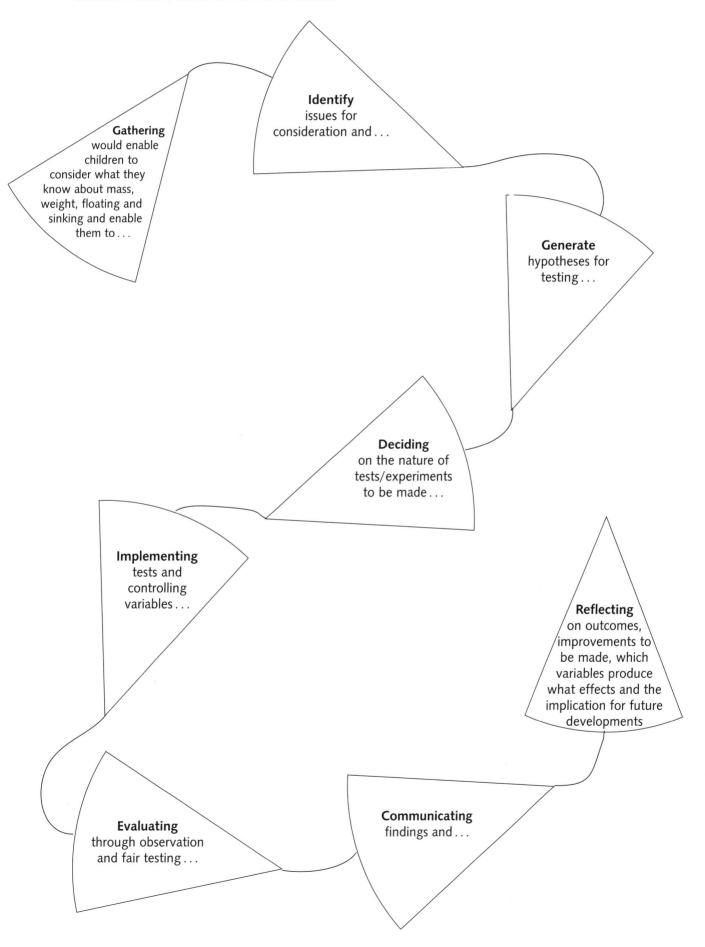

Identify issues for consideration and . . .

Gathering would enable children to consider what they know about mass, weight, floating and sinking and enable them to . . .

Generate hypotheses for testing . . .

Deciding on the nature of tests/experiments to be made . . .

Implementing tests and controlling variables . . .

Reflecting on outcomes, improvements to be made, which variables produce what effects and the implication for future developments

Evaluating through observation and fair testing . . .

Communicating findings and . . .

Lesson 9

Story endings

Part of a story is read or told; the children are asked to provide a credible ending to the story

The children will:
- experience using the complete TASC Problem-solving Wheel
- select from a range of possible endings the most appropriate ending to the story, justifying their choice
- focus on deciding, communicating, evaluating and reflecting

By way of introduction, the teacher shows the children a small, hand painted pottery bell. They are told that the bell has been part of a mysterious story, part of which she is now going to tell the children...

Synopsis of story used in the lesson

A child lives in an old house in the country. Her parents forbid her to go into the room with a blue door, which is situated at the top of the house. Obviously this arouses the child's curiosity and she waits for an opportunity to try to enter the room with the blue door. Seizing the opportunity to see inside the room when both her parents are out, she enters the room and sees that all it contains is a small table on which there is the little pottery hand bell. Going over to the table she picks up the bell and rings it, whereupon . . .

Gathering information

Gather

'What do we know about the story?'

> It's a big house.

> It's a house in the country.

'Who owns the house?'

> It belongs to someone who lives in the town.

'What was the little girl forbidden to do?'

> Don't open the blue door.

> Not to go into the room with the blue door.

> Not to touch anything inside the room.

Generating ideas

'What do you think will happen next?'

> She touched the bell and magic happened.

> The girl fell asleep and dreamt that her mum was dead, but the bell rang and woke her up.

Various other suggestions show that most of the children have their own ideas about the way the story might develop.

The teacher stresses that there is no particular ending to the story. It is a story she has made up and even she does not know how the story will end. Every ending could well be THE ending to the story!

She also stresses that the children need to remember that a good ending will relate to what they know of the story so far; it will be believable, but it will also contain a 'WOW' element – something special that makes it different. Words that will probably give their stories that special 'something' will be the adjectives they choose to describe the action.

Implementing

The children are reminded only to provide the story ending and not attempt to redraft the whole story. Ten minutes is allowed for this part of the activity.

Deciding, communicating and evaluating

Having completed their endings, they return to a plenary to **decide** on the ending they wish the story to have. They are reminded that they will have to give reasons for their choice.

The story endings are laid out around the class for the children to view and consider their choices. The stories are reproduced here with the children's original spelling.

Five children are asked to select an ending. They chose the following:

Ending 1 (Emma Year 2)

...a mackik farie (magic fairy) lived in the bell she was the bautful (beautiful) fare. She aked (asked) the litt (little) grlie (girl) if she wold (would) came to tea the grlie said yes. The little grlie thogt (thought) that the fairy was strasg (strange) wate (what) she had to eat. But when she had tea she thogt it is not bad After all.

(chosen because it was magical)

Ending 2 (Katrina Year 2)

...The ltl gul (girl) did sapd in (was zapped into) the bel and shey whos (was) sged (scared) very much hur mum woc (woke) up and the litl gel cem to noml (normal) and theat (that) wos the end.

(chosen because 'the girl was zapped and it was different')

Ending 3 (Ella Year 2)

...and hur mum hurd the ball and she woc up. Then she got out off bed and then lookt out off the window and she sor the guit (ghost) and she woct (walked) out side and seid wot are you dowing I am picing flaws less go inside it is stating to ran (rain) and wen she whent into the blow (blue) dor was opn and sew woct (walked) up the sters and (the) onmt (ornament - the bell) was gon.

(chosen because of the ghost)

Ending 4 (Mark Year 2)

When she picked the bell up and ringed it a shot of light (lightning) went and she was ded.

(chosen because 'it is *neat* and it is the only one with lightning')

> *In attempting to explain what he meant by the story being 'neat', the teacher notices that the boy concerned is rapidly oscillating the fingers of both hands together in a joining manner, and she comments on this, saying that she can see what he is trying to say by the way he is using his hands to emphasise what he thinks 'neat' means in this context – 'a short, simple but powerfully descriptive ending'.*

Ending 5 (Susan Year 2)

...*wen the grel tust (touched) the bell sucfing (something) magcul (magical) hapud (happened) the bell shruck (shrunk) and mad (made) the grell got biger and biger and biger until sey (she) wos biger then the house. She didt like it sey did (not) now (know) how to get bac to hre (her) nourmil (normal) siz sher muur wos rit (size her mother was right).*

(chosen because the girl grew in size – 'she was a naughty girl')

A vote is taken to see which is the most popular ending. In the end, two stories tie with four votes each – Endings 1 and 5.

Reflecting

In conclusion, the teacher reminds the children that each of the story endings could be the 'right' ending for the story. Each had stemmed from the same starting point: what made the endings different and more or less appealing was the way in which each writer related the ending to the beginning and middle parts of the story, and had created some excitement in the adjectives chosen to make the story ending interesting.

The class **decide** (vote) on the endings they like, deciding which are the most believable conclusions to the story.

The children clearly enjoy this activity, as several comment that they have especially liked listening to other people's story endings; one child in particular is quite euphoric about the way she 'so enjoyed hearing everyone's different stories', another says that, 'listening to everyone else's stories gave me ideas for my own'.

COMMENT ▶

The TASC Wheel provided a good framework for a lesson such as this, which could easily become 'bogged down' at the writing stage.

The important aspects of the learning process were the points at which the children were required to decide and evaluate or justify their reasons for taking particular courses of action.

The writing activity provided a purpose for the reasoning and refinement of creativity through discussion and argument.

Overall reflection on using the TASC Problem-solving Wheel

Although this chapter describes the use of the TASC Wheel over a relatively short space of time in the school (the first half of the autumn term 2001), there is enough evidence to show that the thinking processes that form the TASC Wheel are easily understood by young children. The initial apprehension experienced by the headteacher and writer – that the children would be overwhelmed by the totality of the process – just did not occur, in fact, quite the opposite was apparent. In trying to 'simplify' and spread the introductory process over several sessions – such as only dealing with **gathering information** and **generating ideas** in the early sessions – both teacher and writer felt that the activities were flat and lacking the excitement that was experienced in the later lessons when the whole TASC Wheel process was used.

The quality of thinking comes not so much from the **generation** of ideas, but from the refinement of those ideas that are the products of the **deciding** and **evaluating** aspects of the TASC process.

As the school's original intention was to help develop the children's ability to think creatively, the use of the TASC Problem-solving Wheel has provided a framework or scaffold in which the process of creativity can be developed and refined. The headteacher believes that improvements in written creativity will result from the processes that have stimulated children's powers of reasoning, argument and debate, which are the key elements of the TASC processes of **deciding**, **evaluating** and **communicating**.

A most effective way of encouraging children to engage in the processes of **deciding** and **evaluating** is to place them in a position of having to make and justify choices. In three of the lessons observed (Lessons 7, 8 and 9), the teacher structured the lessons so that choices had to be made.

In these lessons the children were required to select an appropriate design (Lesson 7), or in Lessons 8 and 9, to choose a story ending that was related to the beginning of the story and was the most believable, from a variety of endings that each class had worked on. The decision-making process was carried out by voting or joining a group, the children having been warned previously to be prepared to give reasons for the way they had voted or why they had joined a particular group.

This is not an intimidating or difficult process for the children to experience. In Lesson 8, Roxanne (Year 1) even went so far as to 'publicly' change her mind, having been persuaded to do so by the discussion (**evaluating** and **communicating**) that had taken place.

Emphasis in these sessions was rightly placed on reasoned discussion, in the belief that in due course these processes will produce an improvement in the quality of creative writing.

Children quickly understood the concept of taking responsibility for their choice in this context. 'I chose this because (for these reasons).' They also quickly learnt that the easy answer '...because I like it' is not a satisfactory response because it almost always begs the familiar question '*Why* do you like it?'

One of the reasons why the children quickly learnt to think in this way was because the teacher not only modelled the type of thinking (learning) she wished the children to develop, she also reinforced this process by maintaining an almost continuous commentary on what she was doing and why. This was even the case when she made mistakes or was unable to remember something. The following is typical of this type of commentary:

> 'I think I would choose Mary's story ending because she reminds me of the beginning part of the story. Remember, we said that a good story ending would relate back to the beginning of the story? I also think she has used some interesting adjectives to describe experiences that take place. It's a magical story ending, but I think it is quite believable, don't you? What do you think about that Joanne?'

Or, she guided the children through the various stages of using the TASC Wheel: telling the story of the way the process works, while helping the children to engage in the use of the appropriate terminology and gain an understanding of the meaning of the various stages:

> 'We have **gathered** all these things we know about the story, now let's just remind ourselves what we are trying to do (**identifying the task**), we are trying to find out what would be the best type of boat to carry a heavy elephant. So let's think of lots of ideas about making boats – let's **generate** some ideas about boat making...'

The response to this might be that this is what good teachers do – they model the behaviour they wish to see developed and 'commentate' on what they are doing, i.e. they unfold the story of the learning process for the children to tune into. This is undoubtedly true, but the use of the TASC Wheel provides a secure methodology for *ensuring* that this process happens.

So as not to get bogged down with the more mechanical aspects of the written part of the task (accurate spelling, neat handwriting), the children were only allowed short bursts of time (approximately ten minutes) for producing written responses – the **implementing** aspect of the TASC process. The emphasis at all times in these lessons was on the production of ideas and the justification of any choices made.

Perhaps it was the result of not having too much time to produce written responses that the creation of ideas shines through most of the children's work. No child worried unduly about accurate spelling; all seriously attempted to achieve captivating description.

The Year 1 and Year 2 children's writing, although understandably full of spelling inaccuracies, nevertheless shows a preoccupation with the development of creativity. When the adults present gave help, it tended to focus on helping a child capture in words the idea that he or she was trying to create.

The younger children produced an interesting mix of words and diagrams to portray meaning. Alexander's response as to why the bell had disappeared (Lesson 8) shows an attempt to write, but the diagram says it all: the border around the diagram represents 'the footsteps of the bat coming to steal the bell'.

The one aspect of the TASC Problem-solving Wheel that presented the greatest difficulty to master was the stage to do with **learning** about thinking. Usually, this stage is the final stage of the process coming at the end of a lesson and there may have been occasions when this did not receive the attention it merited because of lack of time. When using this stage, the teacher found that the tendency would be for the children to try to predict what they thought the teacher would like to hear about what they had gained from the activity, rather than what they genuinely had experienced and thought about the process.

The newer version of the TASC Wheel that was used during the latter part of the study replaced **learning** with **reflecting**. This is a far more appropriate term as it allowed for review and contemplation of each of the other stages, providing opportunities for saying what could be improved on the next occasion, or what could have been omitted. The term 'learning' appears to restrict the thinking of children and teacher to thinking about improvement in its narrowest sense.

As with any of the stages of the TASC process, there is no 'right' way to experience thinking, as any stage can be an appropriate place to start or finish. Although the focus of this study was to experience the use of the whole TASC process, familiarity through experience with each of the stages could mean that an entire lesson might be devoted to the development of a set of skills associated with just one of the stages of the TASC Wheel.

Development

The TASC thinking process has been extended across the whole age range of the school, and in literacy is being used to help children develop their writing of fiction, such as the development of characterisation, plot and setting, as well as focusing attention on the development of story openings and 'middles'.

In the non-fictional writing, the TASC Wheel has been used to develop such processes as the writing of instructions, letter writing and report writing.

By the end of the term in which the TASC Wheel was introduced, all the teachers have become familiar with its use. The Reception teacher volunteered the comment that not only has the quality of the children's writing improved as a result of using the TASC thinking processes, the amount they are able to produce has also improved.

As the improvement of children's creative writing was one of the major reasons for deciding to use the TASC Problem-solving Wheel, within one term's use, the school is confident that writing across the age range has improved as a direct result of the use of the TASC processes.

Conclusion

The TASC Problem-solving Wheel provides children with a framework to structure their thinking and expression of their thinking, i.e. writing. Throughout the early stages (described in Lessons 4 to 9), the teacher deliberately shifted the focus of the lessons from producing written outcomes – which might seem to be the logical conclusion where the aim is to improve the quality of children's creative writing – to spending time on the development of the children's questioning, reasoning, imagination and forming of opinions and judgements.

It is a truism to state that children will produce sustained, imaginative, creative writing if they are well motivated and interested in what they are writing about. Bluntly, the teacher explained that, 'It is no good asking children to write unless they have something to write about.' Using the TASC Wheel as a framework to improve writing equips the children with skills that they can call on when they want to write something. They have a systematic procedure for knowing *how* to set about the process of generating material to write about, be it factual or fictional forms of writing.

Children who have learnt how to use the TASC Problem-solving Wheel will know how to set about **gathering** information about what they have to/wish to write about. They will be able to **identify** the nature of the task – to know what is being asked or expected of them. They will be able to **generate** a range of ideas – to explore or find out more about a subject – some or all of which might have a direct bearing on the task in which they are engaged. They will know that they need to return to the task to **identify** what needs to be done, and from the information they have **gathered** and ideas they have **generated**, they will be able to **decide** what it is they are going to write about. At this point they will **implement** the task, i.e. produce a written draft. Having produced a draft, the writing will probably be shared with others as a form of **communication**, at which point there is likely to be some form of **evaluation** of what has been produced, with a discussion about how aspects can be improved or celebrated. The process is incomplete if there is no opportunity for **reflection**, allowing the writer to review the task to see if it has been successfully achieved and has an impact in the way in which it communicates its intentions to other people. What can be done differently or better next time? How can I improve? Where can I improve? What other things do I need to know to be a better writer?

Using the TASC Wheel to Develop Problem-solving and Thinking Skills in Mathematics in the Early Years

LYNNE MCCLURE

Mathematical know-how is the ability to solve problems – not merely routine problems but problems requiring some degree of independence, judgement, originality and creativity.
(Polya 1957)

Where are we now?

Teachers in all phases of education have become expert at adapting to new initiatives. In the early years classroom we have recently taken on board the stepping stones of the Foundation Stage, the adaptations of the National Curriculum found in Curriculum 2000, and the National Literacy and Numeracy Strategies. In mathematics it would be understandable for us to react to the constant need to meet new demands and ever-increasing targets by progressing unimaginatively through the learning objectives of the National Numeracy Strategy (NNS) and 'delivering' a curriculum that is already prescribed. At the same time we are told that there is an absence of cognitive challenge in our mathematics classrooms, that children are rarely asked to use 'higher order' thinking skills or given opportunities to develop the social skills of discussion and collaboration (OFSTED 1994). How then, in a finite timescale, is the early years teacher to resolve the tension between developing children's competency in numeracy, and encouraging them to think in a critical and creative way?

PURPOSE

Of course, many early years teachers do! In the introductory chapter we discussed how many teachers work intuitively within a thinking skills paradigm. The purpose of this chapter is to explore how, in mathematics, we can use a thinking skills Framework that is explicit and part of a whole-school approach. The first part of the chapter sets out the underpinning arguments for such an approach, while later we indicate ways of building on successful practice where it already exists, and suggest ways into working for those who are unfamiliar with the process.

REFLECT

Refer to the audit spiral on the next page which takes the TASC teaching principles and relates them to the teaching of mathematics. Reflect on the skills and strategies you use in your daily mathematics lessons.

Reflect on the Teaching Strategies you use in the Classroom

Are my mental arithmetic questions in the introductory session closed or open or a mixture?

Do I consciously introduce thinking and problem-solving language in every activity?

Do I use as many real-life examples as is possible?

Do I tell the children which skill they are practising and why the skill is important?

Do I model my own thinking strategies in calculating or organising?

Do I provide initial scaffolding such as patterns and stages but withdraw them as soon as the learner demonstrates confidence and competence?

Do I give all the children time to think of an answer?

Do I teach using a problem-solving model that I share with the learners?

Do I use children's errors as key and positive learning points?

Do I plan activities for children to use their own initiative to solve problems?

Do I value unexpected answers?

Do I promote cooperative and social learning as often as possible?

Do I always give feedback to build positive self-image, motivation and independence?

Is the plenary a 'show and tell' opportunity combined with an opportunity to help the children to self-evaluate?

Do I deliberately work on developing a caring and sharing classroom ethos?

So why is it important to emphasise thinking in mathematics?

> Schools can train children to become skilful operators, to perform well in the short term, but this does not develop the network of connections, symbolic representations and meanings which extends the power of thinking and hypothesising.
> (Thumpston 1994)

I know from my work with trainee and practising teachers that they remember learning much of their school mathematics by rote and hence, even as adults, they feel insecure when asked to apply their mathematical knowledge in unfamiliar situations. We need to ensure that our pupils do not suffer the same disadvantage. Pound (1999) describes the responsibility that early childhood educators have to make sure that the 'imperatives of early childhood' are not lost among the noisy demands for early achievement. She draws on the work of Skemp (1989) who talks about two different kinds of learning, both of which are important. The first is 'instrumental learning', in which we learn things by rote, such as the counting numbers, number bonds, etc. The second is 'relational learning', in which we reflect on and think about our learning so that we can apply our mathematical knowledge. We need to ensure that our pupils experience both.

Of course there are certain aspects of number, measurement, shape and space that small children need to know and learn by heart, but successful mathematics teaching needs to be interactive and to involve the children in thinking and doing. They should not be merely passive receivers of information but enthusiastic participants. The work presented to the children must allow them to question ideas, to make choices and decisions, to reflect, and to tolerate uncertainty. The TASC Framework provides opportunities to do all of these things, and to make explicit to the children what and why they are doing them.

REFLECT

Think about your own learning of mathematics:

● What are your memories of your own primary and secondary mathematics?

● Is there an obvious difference between the two, and if so, what would you identify as the significant factors in the difference?

● How confident are you in your own mathematical knowledge now?

● Do you have an understanding of how it all fits together?

● Are there some areas that you really enjoy in mathematics, and if so, why?

● Are there some areas you really don't like, and if so, why?

What's so important about doing it in the early years?

Much has been written about what constitutes an appropriate curriculum for the very young child. Both Atkinson (1992) and Carraher (1991) stress the importance of linking school maths with children's everyday experiences and that we should seek to introduce mathematical systems in contexts that children understand in everyday use. In the Foundation Stage Guidance (QCQ/DfEE 2000) we read 'practitioners should plan opportunities that build on and extend children's knowledge, experiences, interests and skills and develop their self-esteem and confidence in their ability to learn'. Small children, given the chance, are capable of showing an amazing ability to connect the experiences they gain from a wide variety of contexts in order to make mathematical sense of the world. If, on entering formal schooling, they are provided with tasks that seem to bear no relationship to their previous ways of knowing about mathematics, they are likely to feel uncomfortable and may not engage with the tasks at all. The first part of the TASC Problem-solving Wheel allows the children to share their existing knowledge and have it acknowledged, and of course also gives the teacher an insight into their level of understanding.

Play has all the characteristics needed for mathematical thinking: deciding, imagining, reasoning, predicting, planning, trying new strategies and recording. Some play will involve cooperative learning; Bruner suggests that it is while at play that children test their ideas and knowledge in innovative combinations. We now know too that children's understanding of mathematical concepts is not sequential but generative, i.e. they do not need to learn, in order, every single bit of mathematics that they will need to know, but will fit pieces of the jigsaw together given appropriate activities and the opportunity for discussion. So in the early years classroom we can capitalise on these naturally occurring activities and integrate them into more structured tasks.

Talk is important in mathematics at all ages. It is in justifying or explaining our ideas to others that we clarify our own thoughts. Although in the early years we are beginning to encourage children to record their working in mathematics, there should be ample opportunity for talk. For some children this will be the first opportunity they have had to explain what they are doing or how they came to a conclusion. Some will not have been asked for their opinion, ever. Most will find it difficult, but it is important to set up the ethos that talking about their work, and listening to others doing the same, is expected and valued.

What happens when you get to nought?

You have to go virtual, silly.

How should we do it?

In the early years curriculum we have the advantage that most of the mathematics children are expected to learn is easily related to everyday experiences, and should be. There are those who advocate that all mathematics should be taught through 'real-life' problems. However, the ground rules for solving everyday practical numerical or spatial problems and abstract, formal mathematical problems are different. And as children progress through school and the mathematics curriculum, it is often more difficult to relate the formal mathematics they are expected to learn to the informal mathematics they might use everyday. Indeed, many adults find it difficult too! What connection, for example, would you make between solving simultaneous equations and any calculations you would do in the course of everyday life?

Ideally then, the role of the adult in the mathematics classroom is to create a context in which children can make connections between formal and informal mathematics. By making explicit the way in which we approach real-life problems, we can set up an expectation of using thinking skills in all mathematics, so that, later, similar principles can be applied to problems that are more abstract in nature. The beauty of the TASC methodology is that it provides a Framework that is flexible and adaptable to either real life activities or a more abstract investigation. In the previous chapters you have met the principles of the TASC Wheel – let us now consider its application to early years mathematics. As an example, compare how TASC might be applied to both real-life and abstract investigation.

Real-life problem	Abstract investigation
Class needs to make some cakes for the school cake sale	Which number of multilink/unifix can make the most rectangles? (rectangular array)
Learning intentions	
• Approach problems involving number, shape, space and measure in order to identify what they need to do	• Create and describe number patterns • Present results in an organised way • Communicate using informal language

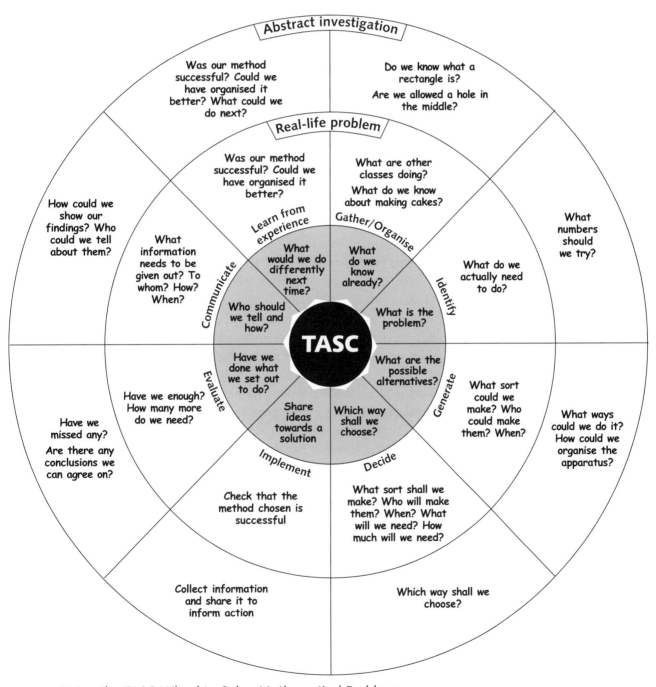

Using the TASC Wheel to Solve Mathematical Problems

Case study of introducing TASC into early years

The school from which the following work is taken – Wootton St Peter's Primary School, Abingdon – had been considering introducing thinking skills into the curriculum for some time, and this was an item on the school development plan. Generally national test results across both Key Stages were good, and the teachers were happy with the results that the children were achieving in their maths SATs. However, the teachers also felt that the children were not operating sufficiently effectively as independent thinkers, and that this was especially evident in the older children. The staff were also concerned to provide those children leaving Key Stage 2 with a range of personal thinking skills that would support them through transition to secondary school and Key Stage 3 itself, to aid the planning for its introduction.

Whole-school INSET (in-service education and training) – including classroom assistants – took place at which different models of a thinking skills curriculum were discussed and evaluated. The staff took the decision to work towards implementing TASC across the whole school. An action plan was launched and subsequently worked upon. It was decided to start with the early years mathematics classes as a pilot and use what was learned to inform future planning for the rest of the curriculum, and for Years 3, 4, 5 and 6. In choosing to use TASC, the early years teachers were enthusiastic about the possibilities of embedding it into the maths curriculum they had already developed. They felt that they were already using many of the strategies contained in the TASC programme, but that these were not made explicit to the children. In mathematics they felt they were using open ended problem-solving to some effect but that, as teachers, they did not *plan* the thinking skills strategies. The school uses a published maths scheme, which they have linked to the Numeracy Strategy and, because they knew the scheme so well, they felt that it would be relatively easy to overlay TASC onto their existing plans. They decided that one way of becoming familiar with TASC was to use the Wheel itself to organise their own planning for its implementation.

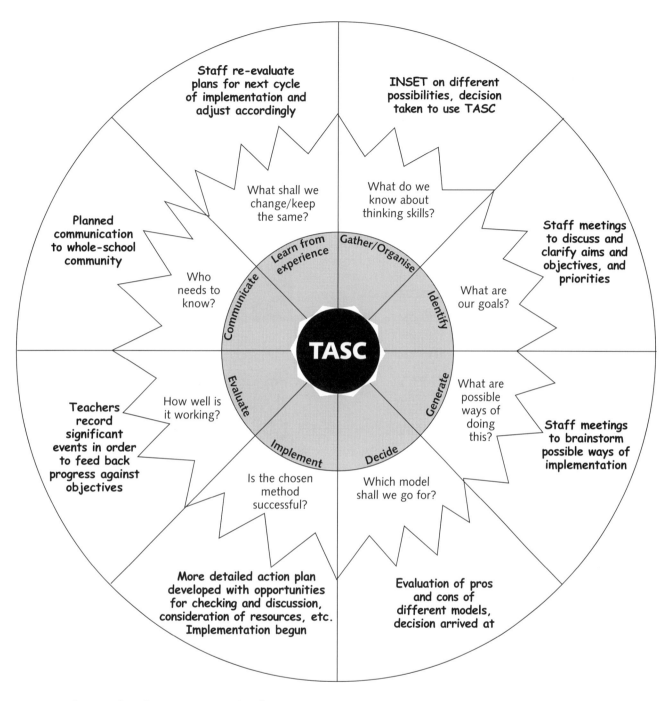

The Teachers' Own TASC Wheel

PURPOSE

As part of the implementation process, the staff spent some time discussing what would be included for each sector of the TASC Wheel, and they brainstormed the sort of questions or statements they would plan to use. The next diagram illustrates the teachers' brainstorm in getting to grips with what they, and the children, should actually be doing within each stage of the Wheel. The diagram was pinned up on the staffroom wall and was added to and amended over time.

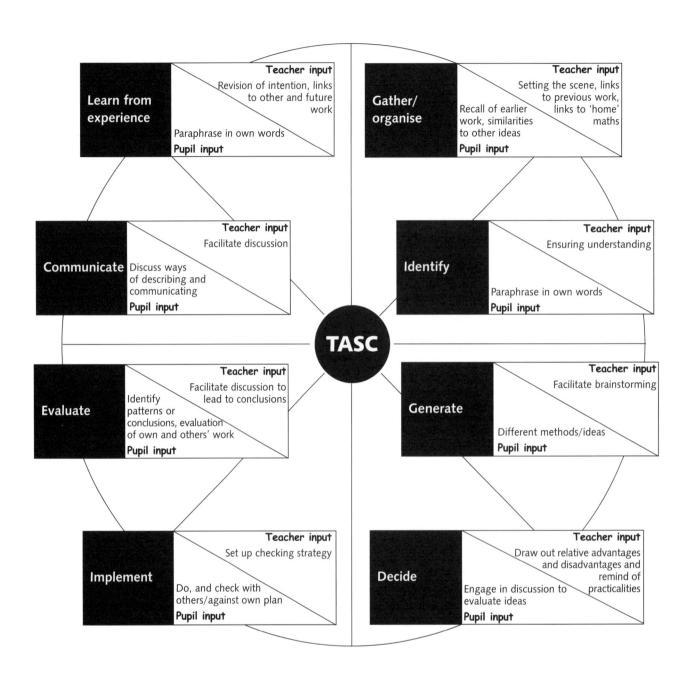

Teachers' Planning TASC Wheel

PURPOSE The following examples are taken from the earliest activities with three classes of children in Reception, Year 1 and Year 2. In each case I have indicated the appropriate learning objectives/intentions, the timescale and a description of what actually happened. Each section is followed by a teacher commentary on the success or otherwise of the activity, and lessons learned.

Activity 1 (Reception)
Class cafe/tea shop

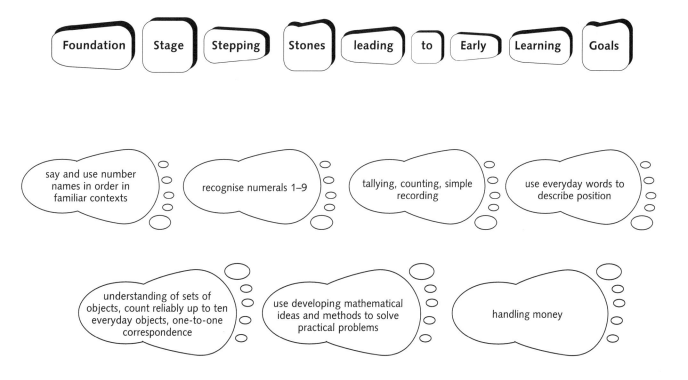

Foundation Stage Stepping Stones leading to Early Learning Goals

say and use number names in order in familiar contexts

recognise numerals 1–9

tallying, counting, simple recording

use everyday words to describe position

understanding of sets of objects, count reliably up to ten everyday objects, one-to-one correspondence

use developing mathematical ideas and methods to solve practical problems

handling money

Timescale

This activity took place over the course of a week's worth of daily maths lessons, each lasting up to threequarters of an hour or so.

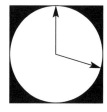

The aspects of the TASC Wheel that were used are shown in the following diagram:

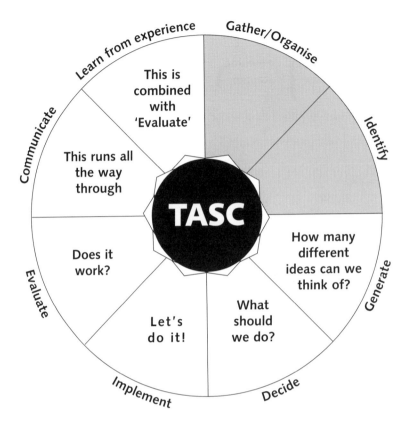

This topic arose because the teacher had been using traditional tales, such as Snow White, the Three Little Pigs, and so on, as a vehicle for counting in the introductory part of the daily maths session. Imaginary play had been encouraged by the provision of basic elements of costume and props. The teacher introduced the idea of reorganising the home corner into a cafe for some of the characters they had met so far. She invited ideas of possible activities/arrangements from the children in turn and explained that they would brainstorm possibilities first and then look at each in more detail before deciding on exactly what they would do. She wrote each down briefly on a flip-chart but did not comment, other than encourage the children to explain a little more if needed.

What could we do?

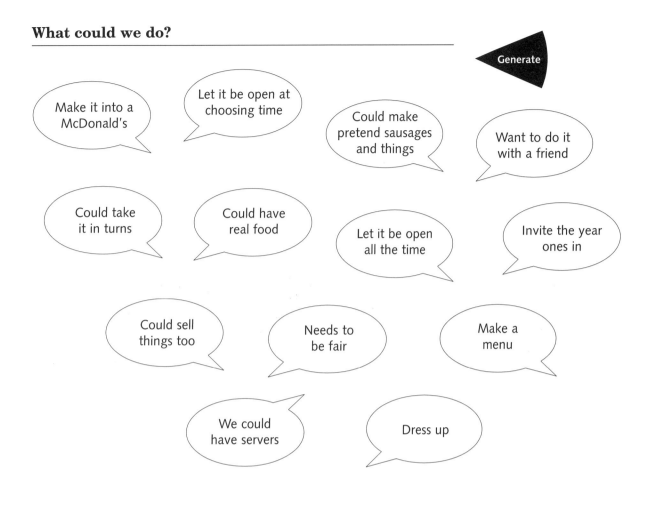

Which is the best idea to try first?

The teacher then explained that there were a lot of good ideas and they couldn't do them all, so they had to find a way of deciding what to do. Each idea was discussed and the children were encouraged to think about the implications of each. They decided that the first thing they had to do was get the cafe ready for use, and after that they could use it at choosing time as well as in the maths sessions. They made a list of all the jobs that would have to be done and discussed how they could make sure everyone did an equal share. They listed all the things they would need.

What jobs to get it ready?

Clear out the home corner and set up the table and chairs

Sort out clothes to wear

Signs

Make an open and closed sign with the time on it and a clock

Make pretend food (real food was rejected on terms of hygiene and cost)

Sort out the tablecloths and plates, cutlery, and so on

Sort out the money

Make a price list

Implement

Putting our ideas into action

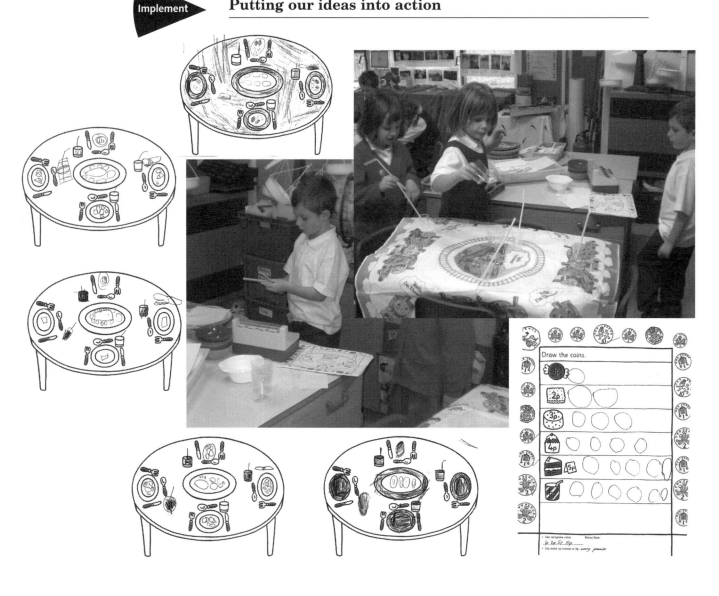

The small maths groups took it in turn, during the daily maths sessions, to do one of the 'jobs' on the list to prepare the cafe. This required negotiation and occasional intervention by the teacher or another adult. The children, at various times, discussed how to make sure all the playdoh cakes were the same size (they decided to use balances), the relative prices of the items, what time the open/closed sign should say, how they should set the table, how many people should be allowed at any one time to be in the cafe. In each plenary the children who had been working on the cafe preparation would report back on how much they had done and suggest what the next group should do. In parallel with this activity, other children in the class were working within the published scheme, on activities that supported, and were supported by, the cafe experience.

Once the cafe was ready the children used it in maths sessions and at choosing time. They decided which traditional tale characters the patrons were going to be and the waiters/ waitresses set the table accordingly.

The seven dwarves
7

The three bears
3

Does it work? What have we learned?

Once the cafe was in operation, the children discussed things they had enjoyed doing or new ideas they had used in the plenary session. This process of evaluation was combined with **Learn from experience**, and some changes were made as the project progressed.

Teacher's comments

Although the initial idea itself was rather contrived, the children were happy to go along with it. I was pleasantly surprised at the range of suggestions that initially emerged, but found it difficult to allow the children sufficient time to think around the issue without rushing them on to the next stage, once they had produced the ideas I had been hoping for! The discussion of which ideas were good or difficult to implement was harder to control. As Reception children they were obviously not used to listening to and considering others' opinions, and I needed to intervene and guide the process quite tightly.

I was impressed by the wide range of mathematical language that was employed in the discussions, both in the preparation stage and in the live café. Eavesdropping on conversations about time, for example, indicated that some of the children had a very clear idea of the passing of time, and the appropriate opening and closing times for a shop. In making playdoh food, some of the children were very keen that the small cakes should be the same size if they were going to cost the same. After much discussion they used the balances to check that the amount of playdoh being used was the same.

Although only one or two children understood the concept of using the scales, their expertise was readily accepted and built upon by the other children in the group. The classroom is arranged so that all resources are available to the children, and I felt that this enabled the children to be more creative in their ideas.

As a first attempt at using TASC, I felt that it had given a structure to the project, which was certainly beneficial to me. The next stage will be to remind the children of the order in which they approached the topic and to make the stages explicit in the next activity, introducing to the children the sections of the Wheel that are appropriate.

Activity 2 (Year 1)
Explode a number

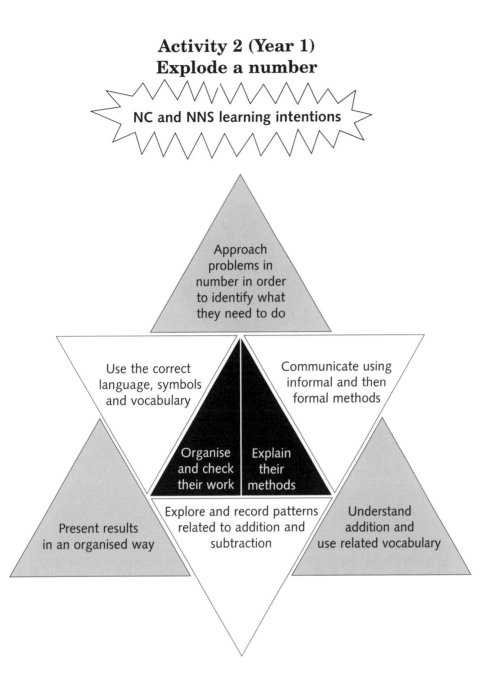

NC and NNS learning intentions

Approach problems in number in order to identify what they need to do

Use the correct language, symbols and vocabulary

Communicate using informal and then formal methods

Organise and check their work

Explain their methods

Present results in an organised way

Explore and record patterns related to addition and subtraction

Understand addition and use related vocabulary

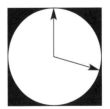

Timescale

This activity, which took three daily maths lessons to complete, is intended to consolidate number bonds and provide an opportunity for exploring pattern. It began each day as a whole-class activity and then children had the opportunity to work with a partner, or alone, before coming back together as a whole class at the end of each session.

This was the first time the children had been introduced to the TASC Wheel. The teacher explained that this was going to help them to be more organised in their work. She referred to it as each part of the activity took place and the aspects of the TASC Wheel were introduced.

Gather &
organise

Gathering and organising what we know

This was not a new activity to the children; they were used to the idea of a special number for the day and had already begun to contribute objects to the interactive display that the teacher had started. The teacher introduced the idea of a new special number for the day – in this case, 6 – and asked 'What do we already know about 6?

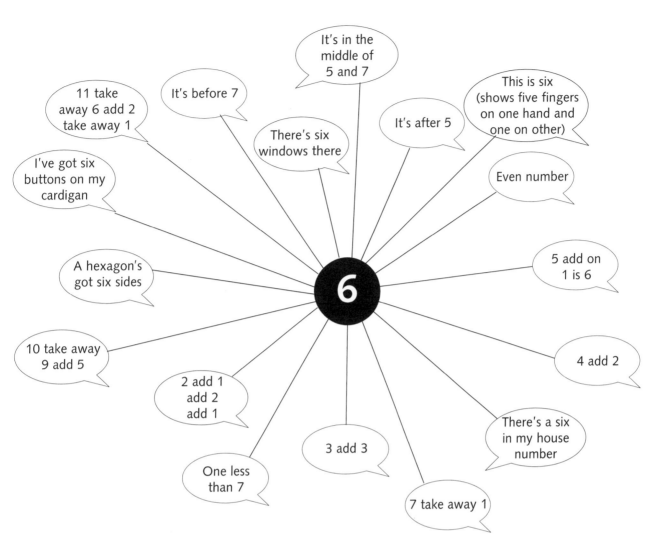

Gather/organise

What are we trying to do?

Identify

The teacher checked that the children understood what they were being asked to do, i.e. find out everything they could about the number 6; and make or draw or write about their ideas.

What ideas shall we put into action?

Decide & Implement

Working in pairs the children made/drew/recorded their own ideas. This produced various 3D models using six unifix, polydrons, etc., 2D pictures such as houses with six windows, animals with six legs, and some children began more formal recording showing six on the number line or writing simple additions.

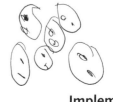

Implement

Communicating, evaluating and reflecting

In the plenary, these three stages of the TASC Wheel were combined as the children offered suggestions and comments that the teacher reflected back, making links between ideas where possible and asking which the children thought were especially interesting and why.

Day 2

Gathering and organising what we already know

The teacher brought out the differences between pictures and number sentences, translated where appropriate and reminded the children of relevant vocabulary and symbols.

What are we going to do today?

The children paraphrased the learning intention.

How could we do it?

The teacher again drew attention to the variety of apparatus available, modelled an example and asked for others.

What do we need to think about?

The children worked with a partner to generate number sentences.

$$2+2+2 \qquad 3+3 \qquad 5+4$$

$$6+0$$
$$6-0$$

$$0-0$$
$$10-0$$
$$50-1$$
$$30-0$$

$$0-0$$
$$10-4$$
$$9-3$$
$$8-2$$
$$7-1$$

$$1+1+1+1+1+1$$

Implement

Communicating, evaluating and reflecting

In the plenary the children offered suggestions, some of which were recorded onto the flip-chart. The teacher asked for comments on anything interesting or any patterns that anyone had found. A heated discussion took place about whether they had found all the addition bonds or whether you could go on for ever. Joe said that you could go on adding for ever if you made the things you were adding smaller and smaller. They couldn't come to any conclusion about subtraction, which only some children had used.

Day 3

Gathering knowledge and identifying links

The teacher helped the children to recall what they had done yesterday and asked them to think for a while before choosing a number with which to repeat the activity. Again she drew the children's attention to apparatus they might choose to use. She also suggested that if they thought they had spotted a pattern, they should write it down in a way that other people could see it. This time the children worked alone.

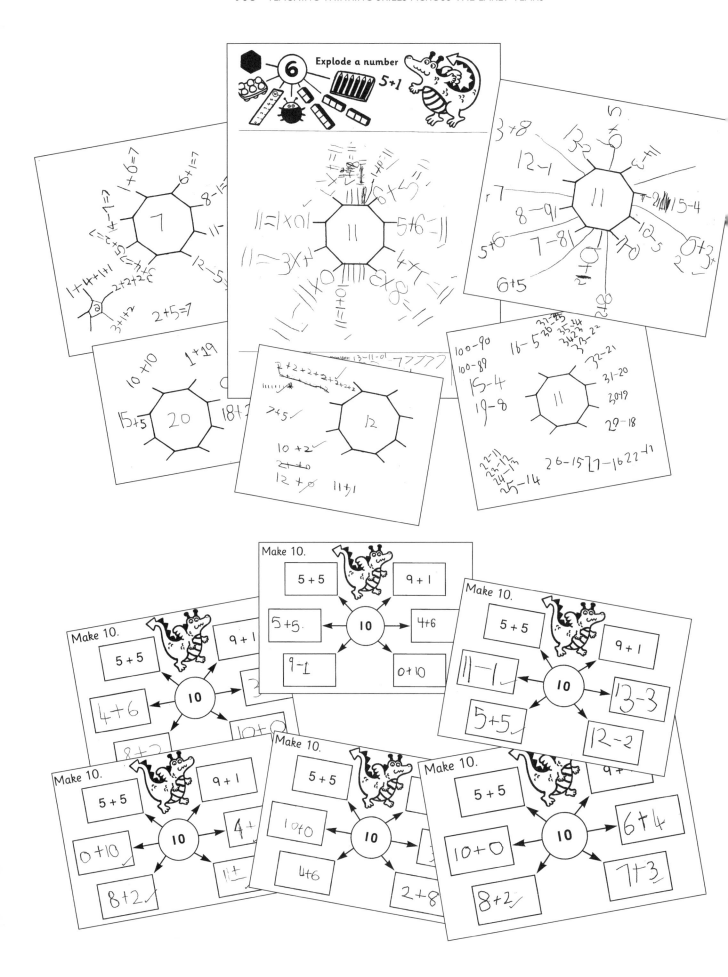

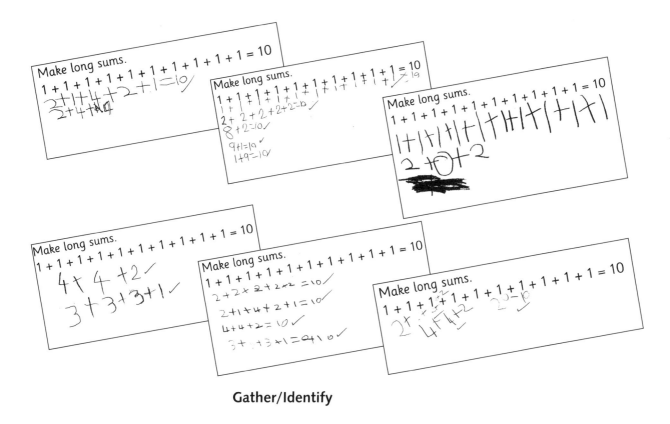

Gather/Identify

What action shall we take to check our progress?

Most of the children preferred to use apparatus to help them to write their number sentences and most were happy to work only with addition. However, there were a minority of children for whom the apparatus was a distraction and they were much more interested in the patterns they could produce in the computation.

Communicating, evaluating and reflecting

Again in the plenary the children shared what they had found out. Those who had discovered patterns were encouraged to explain what they had noticed and if possible, to give some generalisation.

Teacher's comments

The children were used to this sort of activity but not the more structured way of introducing it. The wide range of ability was more evident as the activity progressed and by Day 3 the patterns that some of the children shared were incomprehensible to those who were still at the stage of recording their practical partitioning activities. However, every child discovered something and their contributions were valued.

In the more able group, there were some wonderful leaps of understanding. Joe decided that addition was boring and subtraction held many more possibilities. He used a 1-20 number line to generate a pattern that gave a difference of 11 and then declared that boring too. When I challenged him to find some subtraction sentences that began with a number larger than 20, he took a 100 number square and counted back from 100. The dislocation of line in the number square caused him some difficulty to begin with but he mastered it and then began generating 100-89, 99-88, 98-87, and so on. He used no counting apparatus other than the number line and square.

Referring to the TASC Wheel was helpful in reminding the class of the focus of the discussion. After this the unused bits of the Wheel will be explained and for each subsequent activity, I intend to emphasise the parts of the TASC Wheel that will be useful.

Activity 3 (Year 2)
Sorting boxes

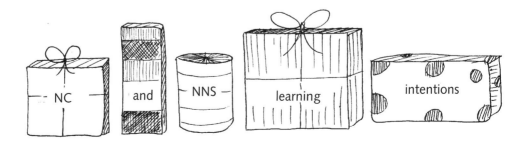

By Year 2 we can begin to use the whole of the TASC Wheel and make all its stages explicit. It is easy to make connections between the learning intentions of the NNS or NC and the different sectors of the Wheel.

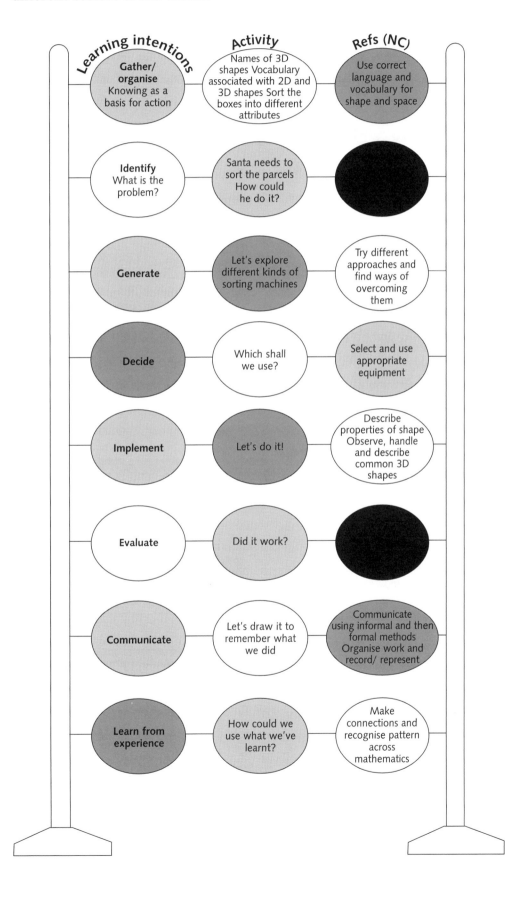

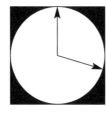

Timescale

This activity again was related to the published scheme that the school uses in Key Stage 1. The topic was seasonal, too. It took place over one week's worth of daily mathematics lessons. This was the first time the children had been introduced to the TASC Wheel.

Day 1

Introducing the TASC Wheel

Whereas the teachers in Reception and Year 1 had decided to introduce the TASC Wheel at the end of the first activity, the Year 2 teacher chose to spend some time talking about it before using it. She explained that this way of working was going to help them to become more organised in their thinking, and would also help them when they got stuck. She asked the children to suggest an everyday problem to use as an example so that they could see how the TASC Wheel worked. They decided on the problem they had with parents parking dangerously outside the school. They very briefly worked through the TASC Wheel, and discussed what form of thinking they were using at each stage.

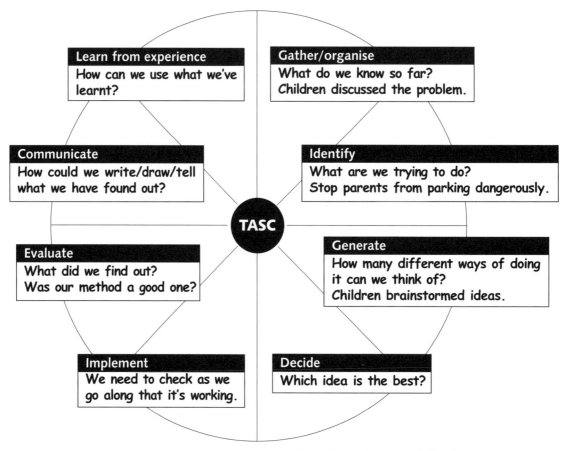

Using the TASC Wheel for the First Time

Day 2

Gathering and organising what we know

Gather & organise

The teacher had prepared a variety of different 3D shapes, which were either cubes or cuboids. The children were asked what they knew about them, discussed the characteristics of each, rehearsed the relevant vocabulary and decided which was which.

The teacher then produced some parcels, again cubes or cuboids, wrapped in various sorts of Christmas wrapping papers and some with ribbons and bows. The children were asked to think of questions that would sort the parcels into two even or uneven groups. They tried each one to see if it would work and if successful, the teacher recorded it on a card.

Does it have square faces?	Is it a cuboid?	Is it stripey?
Does it have a bow?	Is it heavy?	Is it gold?
Is it big?	Is it long?	Is it plain?
Is it blue?	Does it have tinsel?	

Day 3

Identifying problems and generating solutions

The teacher explained that Santa had lots and lots of presents to give to children, but the children's names had come off. All he had was a list to say what each person's present was like. He wanted some help to make a machine that would sort all the presents so that each child would receive the right one. A discussion of what a possible sorting machine might look like took place as the children recalled earlier sorting activities they had done and made links to the questions generated the day before.

A small group then began the activity while the rest of the class worked in parallel on 3D and sorting activities taken from the published scheme. Each group was provided with multiple copies of the questions and yes/no cards. Their aim was to make a machine that would sort the presents in as quick a way as possible.

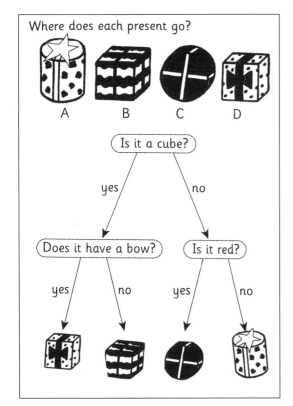

Draw their friends.

How many? 6

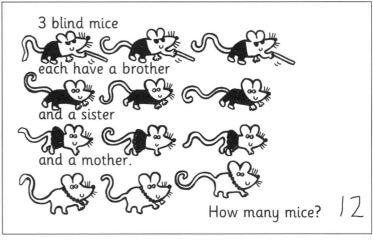

3 blind mice
each have a brother
and a sister
and a mother.

How many mice? 12

Days 4 and 5

Other groups did the activity on subsequent days. Each group kept a record of their machine by sticking the questions onto paper. On Day 5, the children took it in turn to describe their machines and evaluate their own and those of the other groups, before suggesting improvements.

The teacher then referred back to the TASC Wheel and made links between what they had been doing and the sectors of the Wheel.

Teacher's comments

As the other teachers had indicated, the Wheel was certainly a useful planning tool for us all. As a first example of using the TASC Wheel, I felt it had been reasonably successful but that it needed to be modelled consistently during mathematics investigations before the children would take it as a model they could use themselves. The activity was a self-checking one in that it was evident if the machine worked or not. The evaluation time provided an opportunity for me to help the children to make generalisations. In the sector 'Learning from experience' the children suggested lots of other sorting machines they could make and some of them chose to do this in choosing time on subsequent days.

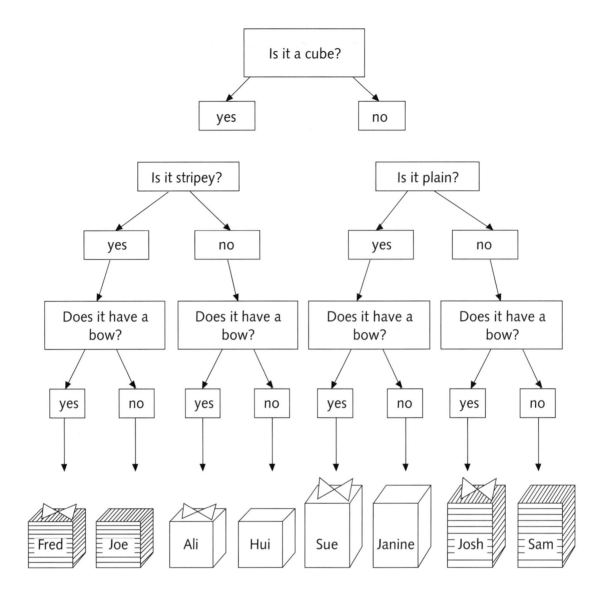

 **COMMENT** ▶ The examples above were those taken from the very beginning of introducing the TASC Wheel. The teachers felt that they had made a positive start but that it would only be possible to evaluate the success of the strategy after half a term or so. With smaller children the emphasis was on modelling the stages in the Wheel. Developing the strategy across the whole school and curriculum should ensure that in the older years the modelling would have been rehearsed frequently enough for the children to become more independent in its use.

The conclusions the teachers came to as they planned further use of TASC were that:

● the Wheel should be prominent in the classroom and that the children should be a part of generating the symbols and vocabulary that would help them to interpret it;

● not all parts of the Wheel are relevant all the time and it can be used flexibly;

- for younger children it is important to repeatedly refer to the Wheel and model the different forms of thinking in an informal way;

- TASC was easily amalgamated into the existing maths curriculum, for both real-life problems and more abstract investigations;

- for older children, explicit skills could possibly be introduced using several sections rather than the whole TASC Wheel. Although, ideally, opportunities should be sought for the introduction of the whole Wheel;

- as the TASC Wheel was used across more subject areas and classrooms, there would be opportunities to explore it with the whole school.

The TASC Wheel provides children with an element of choice in their studying. Ensuring that the primary classroom is a place where children can take responsibility for their learning is very important, especially in mathematics where, as I have suggested before, many adults feel disempowered by the teaching methods they have experienced. Encouraging children to take risks in a structured and supportive environment is vital too, if they are to build up an academic resilience that will ensure they don't give up when the going becomes more difficult.

The TASC Wheel also provides children with an opportunity to demonstrate their thinking in a way that is not always possible in classrooms where there is an emphasis on recording. We know that assessment should be built-in not added-on, and providing children with opportunities to discuss and explain their work rather than only writing it down is a more reliable way of finding out what a child can do and understand.

Michael Pohl (1997), an established Australian writer in thinking skills, suggests that a 'thinking school' embodies a thinking culture that will:

● empower children with the language, tools and strategies to engage in a wide variety of analytical, critical and creative thinking tasks;

● provide on-going opportunities for developing, practising and refining skills of thinking;

● provide instruction and practice in ways of managing, organising and recording data;

● engage children in the higher order thinking skills of analysis, synthesis, and evaluation;

● assist in the transfer of skills to everyday life and everyday situations as tools for lifelong learning.

For many teachers, the 'using and applying' part of the maths National Curriculum has often proved difficult. For some time there was debate in the mathematics education community about whether there should be a separate attainment target concerned with application so that teachers would have to be seen to be planning to do it; or whether it should be embedded within the other attainment targets with the danger of it being sidelined. While it is true that some older students of mathematics enjoy it for its own intrinsic beauty, for the vast majority, mathematics will be a tool for life. I hope that in reading about the teachers and children who are at the beginning of their work with TASC, you will be encouraged to try it in your own classroom, and help produce the mathematicians of the future.

> We are all of us, at all ages, skilled mathematicians. We just haven't often learned it in our mathematics lessons.
>
> (Lewis 1996)

Using the TASC Wheel to Maximise Children's Thinking and Problem-solving in Early Years Science

NICOLA BEVERLEY

Introduction

> ### *NC Programmes of Study reference*
>
> Sc1: During KS1 children observe, explore and ask questions about living things, materials and phenomena. They begin to work together to collect evidence to help them answer questions and to link this to simple scientific ideas. They evaluate evidence and consider whether tests or comparisons are fair. They use reference materials to find out more about scientific ideas. They share their ideas and communicate them using scientific language, drawings, charts and tables.

Note: I would like to thank the following teachers who collectively have contributed to this chapter: Janice Carder, St Mary's RC Primary School, Lincs. (Headteacher: Katherine Doherty); Sue Staniland: The Tedder Primary School, Lincs. (Headteacher: Christine Reeve); Helen Challinor, Stickney Primary School, Lincs. (Headteacher: Chris Holmes); Rachel Bensley and Lisa Gordon: Gonerby Hill Foot CE Primary School, Lincs. (Headteacher: Peter Riches).

Thanks also to Little Gonerby CE Infant School, Lincs., and Barrowby CE Primary School, Lincs., for providing the photographs used in this chapter.

A deluge of strategies, legislation and documentation have in recent years done much to cause teachers in primary schools to question the effectiveness of their approaches to the teaching of science.

In Foundation Stage classrooms, the introduction of the Early Learning Goals for children's learning has reinforced thematic and experiential approaches to the teaching of science skills, knowledge and understanding of very young children. In Key Stage 1, on the other hand, teachers frequently feel constrained by a reduction of time available for science and the perceived limitations of both programmes of study and the DfEE/QCA Schemes of Work for Science (2000). In reality, although undoubtedly time remains an issue, both sets of documentation do much to reinforce the importance of practical, hands-on experiences as a fundamental part of early science learning.

The TASC Problem-solving Framework reinforces the way in which children learn as they experience effective science teaching. The Sc1 programmes of study in particular mention skills that children should be taught, which echo those of the TASC paradigm.

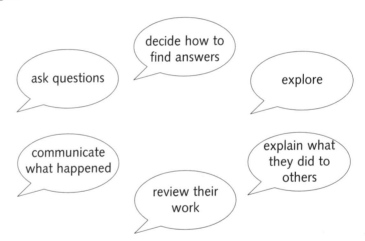

It is in the early years that children acquire an extensive range of essential scientific and thinking skills that will provide them with valuable tools for learning throughout their education.

PURPOSE The purpose of this chapter is to explore how young children's learning in science can be enhanced and extended through the application of the TASC Problem-solving Framework and the development of a range of key Tools for Effective Thinking.

REFLECT Many of the strategies and ideas included may well be familiar. However, taking time to reflect on what we currently do in order to extend our practice, enables us to develop our skills further.

Facilitating children's use of thinking and problem-solving skills will bring tremendous benefits, leading to raised attainment for all children.

Developing key thinking skills

Children, from their earliest days in school, need to be given frequent opportunities to communicate their own ideas about the world, themselves and the way things work.

What children communicate about their thinking both before and after a science lesson, an investigation, enquiry or unit of work provides teachers with much information about the state and stage of their learning.

- Knowing what children already 'know' and have firmly in place will help avoid unnecessary repetition within learning experiences.

- Misconceptions may be revealed, allowing information to be used formatively by teachers in future planning.

- Knowing what children have 'learned' will provide evidence of progress made and useful assessment information about the next steps needed to take their learning further.

- Do you give children in your class the opportunity to contribute their ideas about science freely, sharing what they know or think they know about a particular topic?

- Do you provide an environment where children feel sufficiently confident to say what they think without fear of unhelpful correction of ideas that are 'wrong' or of negative responses from their peers?

Throughout this chapter strategies will be described that might be used in improving children's abilities to think about science and to communicate that thinking. Real examples will be given of how these strategies have been incorporated within teachers' planning and in the practical learning experiences of children in four Lincolnshire schools: St Mary's RC Primary School, The Tedder Primary School, Stickney Primary School, and Gonerby Hill Foot CE Primary School.

 Do you use any of these thinking tools in your classroom currently?

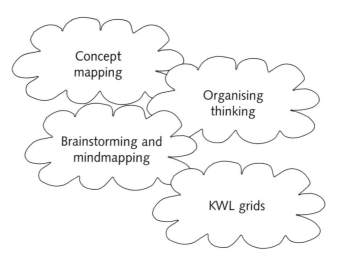

Concept mapping

Concept mapping or mindmapping is a thinking tool that helps children to recognise how ideas (concepts) link together. The mapping process itself consolidates and reinforces learning, effecting a wider and deeper understanding of science. For younger children, maps should be kept relatively simple, containing only a few concepts and significant links. Concept words usually describe an object, for example a leaf or plant, or an event such as growing or flowering. A concept word should always produce a picture in your mind.

- Learning in science can be fragmented because of the nature of the science curriculum, broken up as it is into discrete programmes of study, Sc2, 3 and 4 – Biology, Chemistry and Physics.

- How often do we as teachers help children to recognise the links between learning that occur during one unit of science work and another? For example, the idea that magnetism is a force, learned during a 'materials' topic, and that pushes and pulls or friction are forces, learned during a unit about the playground.

● PURPOSE   Concept mapping can be used at either the beginning or end of a unit of work (or both).

The thinking process:

- helps children bring back into their working memory what they already know (or think they know) about a particular topic;

- encourages children to think about possible links between ideas and words within a topic, improving the depth of their understanding;

- reveals any misconceptions in terms of what children know and understand at that point. This allows the teacher to address issues raised in a planned and systematic way through later work;

- becomes an effective assessment tool when children produce a map before and then one after a unit of work, revealing what has been learned. An initial map may be added to or altered (using a different colour pen or pencil), again revealing what has been learned.

How to do it

- With very young children, begin with the whole class and use a practical, hands-on approach to creating a map.

- Make a set of flash cards of concept words (and/or pictures) linked to the current science topic.

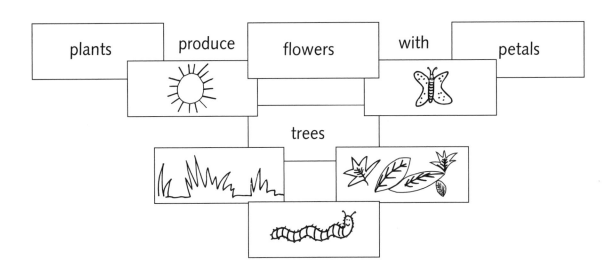

- Ask some of the children to hold a flash card each.
- Discuss with the class where they think there might be links between words and/or pictures, e.g. plant and flower.
- When a definite link has been made, give each child a piece of string or wool to mark the link.
- Write phrases that describe each link on pieces of card or paper and 'peg' them onto the string link.
- Continue until all concept words/pictures have been discussed and linked.

- As children become more experienced with the process, introduce pencil and paper recording of maps.

Remember to:
- provide a basic word list to support children as they begin to map their ideas;
- use 'thinking partners' so that children can bounce ideas off one another;
- begin with the whole class and model the process;
- demonstrate how to link key words with lines and a few words describing the link:

| plants | produce | flowers | with | petals |

Concept map (before block of work)

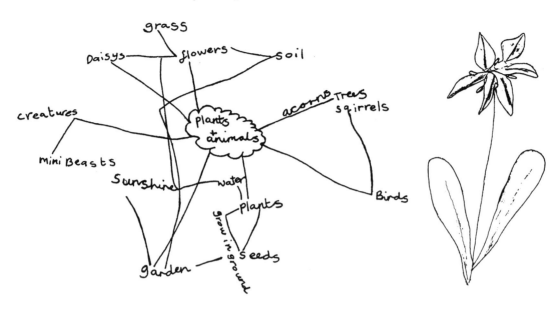

Children were asked to think of anything they knew about plants and animals.

Concept map (after block of work)

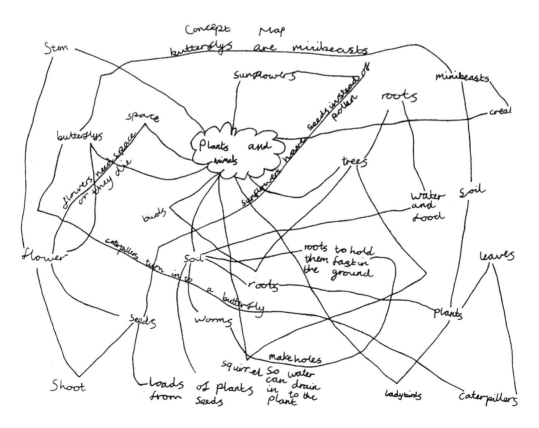

Children reflected on what they had learned and were able to identify numerous links between aspects of the topic. (Note how an unusual misconception was revealed.)

Winter

What do we already know about this?

The children brainstormed what they already knew about winter. They offered a range of ideas and these were listed by the teacher on a flip-chart.

What do you know already about winter?

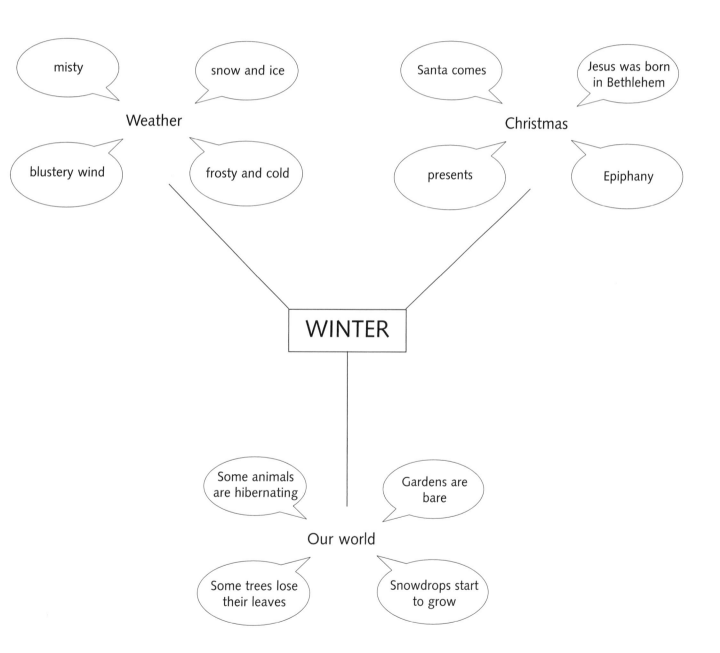

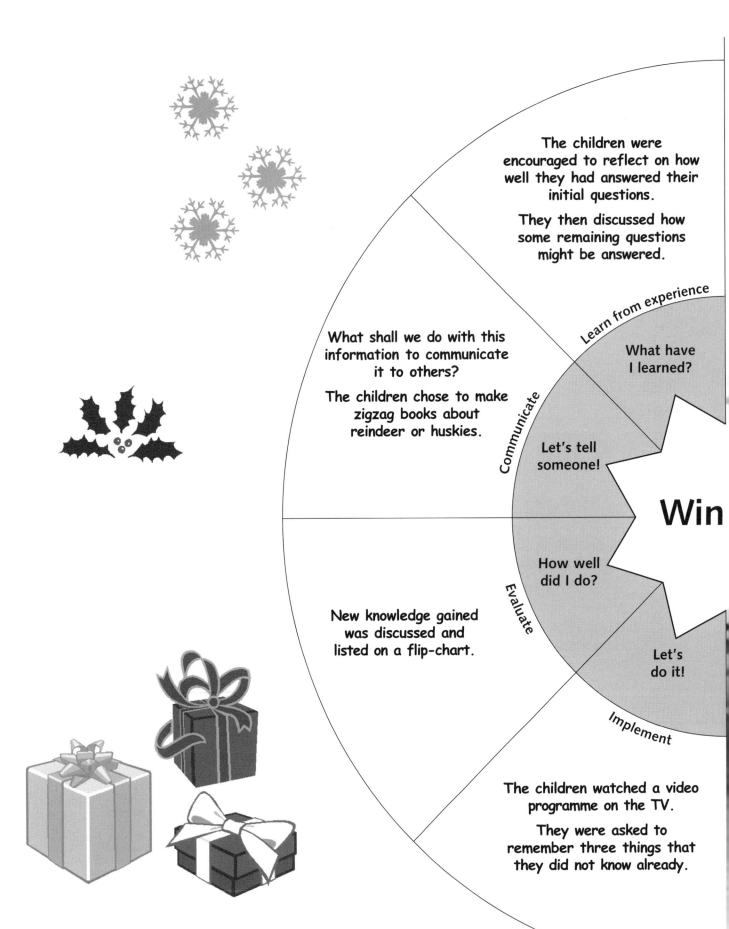

The children were encouraged to reflect on how well they had answered their initial questions.

They then discussed how some remaining questions might be answered.

Learn from experience

What have I learned?

What shall we do with this information to communicate it to others?

The children chose to make zigzag books about reindeer or huskies.

Communicate

Let's tell someone!

Win

How well did I do?

Evaluate

New knowledge gained was discussed and listed on a flip-chart.

Let's do it!

Implement

The children watched a video programme on the TV.

They were asked to remember three things that they did not know already.

A summary of the TASC stages involved in a project on 'Winter'

The children brainstormed what they already knew.

They offered a range of ideas, which were listed on a flip-chart.

Gather/organise

What do I know about this?

What is the task?

Identify

- To recall current knowledge.
- To identify questions to answer.
- To extend knowledge of aspects of Winter and answer questions.

ter

How many ideas can I think of?

Generate

The children came up with a list of questions they would like to find the answer to.

Which is the best idea?

Decide

They thought about how they might find the answers to their questions.

What is it that we want to find out?

The teacher established clear learning objectives for the lesson. These included:

● To recall existing knowledge and understanding of winter.

● To identify questions to explore.

● To answer questions and extend knowledge and understanding of aspects of winter.

G H F	Date 12.1.01	Curriculum Area *Science - Winter*	Cross-curricular/PSHE links
POS *2a*		Learning Objective *To recall what they know about Winter and extend their knowledge*	*Geography*
Introduction *Brainstorm what the children know about Winter. Ask what they would like to know about Winter. Discuss how they could find out more information about Winter.*			Vocabulary *Winter, Season, Jack Frost, huskies*
Main Activity *Put the information on a mindmap. Watch the video 'Winter.' Ask the children if there was anything on the video that they did not know before. Write it onto the mindmap.*			Extension
			Support
Plenary *Talk about their favourite Winter activity.*			Resources *Video - Winter*
Notes/Implications for future planning *The children showed a good knowledge of Winter during the discussion before the video and thought about what they would like to know and where they could find out the information.*			Key Assessment *To extend their knowledge of Winter*

Teacher's lesson plan

What questions would we like to answer?

The children came up with a list of questions about winter they would like to find the answer to.

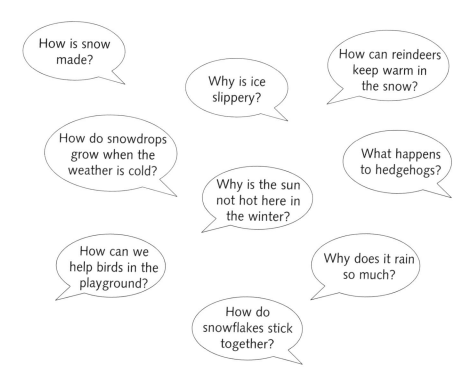

How is snow made?

Why is ice slippery?

How can reindeers keep warm in the snow?

How do snowdrops grow when the weather is cold?

What happens to hedgehogs?

Why is the sun not hot here in the winter?

How can we help birds in the playground?

Why does it rain so much?

How do snowflakes stick together?

Comment

Children should be taught how to use a range of methods of finding information (evidence) to answer their questions.

They must also be given plenty of opportunity to take the method they have been taught, practise it and finally apply it within a new context.

For example: Teach the skill of using an index in an information book (during a literacy lesson), practise and apply the skill during a science lesson, investigating what birds need to survive winter weather.

How can we answer our questions?

They thought about how they might find answers to their questions.

Their suggestions included:

Implement

Let's do it!

The children watched a video about how different animals are adapted to a winter environment. They were asked to remember three things that they didn't know already.

> *Comment*
>
> Children should be taught how to use a range of methods of finding information (evidence) to answer their questions.
>
> They must also be given plenty of opportunity to take the method they have been taught, practise it and finally apply it within a new context.
>
> For example: Teach the skill of using an index in an information book (during a literacy lesson), practise and apply the skill during a science lesson, investigating what birds need to survive winter weather.

Other possible ways of helping the children to find answers to these questions might include:

- asking a member of a local wildlife group or the RSPB to talk about hedgehogs in winter or caring for wild birds;

- providing a structured opportunity for children to explore a useful website or CD-ROM and find information to answer their questions.

Did we answer our questions?

New knowledge gained was discussed and listed on the flip-chart.

What did we find out that we didn't know already?

What shall we do with this information to communicate it to others?

Literacy link

The children worked in groups to make zigzag books explaining what they had learned.

Some individuals produced illustrations while others wrote simple sentences by hand or using IT. Each group produced a contents page and index, a cover and blurb for their book.

Children might also communicate their findings through 'hot seating'.

The hot seat

Group members nominate a specialist area they have learned about, e.g. birds in the winter. A volunteer from each group takes up the 'hot seat' and other children ask them questions about their specialism.

What have we learned?

   Encourage children to reflect on how well they answered their initial questions. Discuss how the remaining questions might be answered.

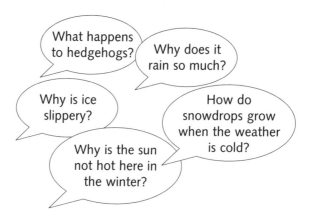

As an extension or homework activity, challenge the children to take a question and see if they can find out any information for themselves – encouraging parents to become involved, developing the use of their local library, and so on.

Organising thinking

When children are first introduced to this method of organising their thinking they will need ample support through teacher modelling and supportive interaction. As confidence grows children will use the method as a thinking tool, increasingly unassisted, in a variety of contexts and across the curriculum.

How to do it

We all think better when we can 'bounce' ideas off one another. Reflect on instances when you have worked with a colleague or friend on a specific project, presentation or written report. How useful did you find your 'thinking partner' in helping to clarify, structure, prioritise and organise, etc. your thoughts?

- Children should work in pairs with a 'thinking partner'.

- Provide 'Post-it Notes' (or similar) so that words and thoughts can be grouped and regrouped.

- Share the subject with the children and encourage initial ideas through questions such as 'What do we know about frogs?'

- Then ask the children to think of two items – words, ideas or 'facts' – about frogs.

frogs have webbed feet

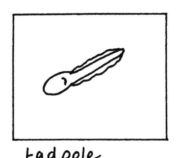

tadpole

- Allow two to five minutes for thinking partners to talk and agree which two they will record before asking them to draw a picture or symbol representing the item or to write it down.

- Call time and ask each pair in turn to bring their Post-it Notes up to the front and to stick them on the whiteboard or flip-chart.

- Ask each pair to explain what their two items are as they display them.

● When all contributions have been collected ask the children to come up with ways in which they might sort out the resulting 'mess' of words and ideas.

 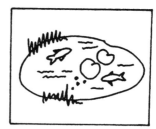

For example, 'in water', 'under bushes', and a picture of a pond might be grouped together under the heading 'HABITAT' (write the word and explain its meaning in simple terms).

● Work through the collection with children, systematically grouping, removing duplicates, leaving any that do not fit (or reveal misconceptions) until the end of the process.

● Children should then be asked what they think should be done with the 'misfits'. Any misconceptions should provide a focus for individual or whole-class/group teaching at a later date – that is, if peer discussion does not provide the stimulus children need to reconstruct the misconception.

For example, 'frogs eat fish'. Do they? How might we find out whether they do or not? Can you think of a way to find an answer?

● Over time and with lots of practice, this method of organising thinking becomes a powerful tool for children. So much so that eventually they will use it spontaneously and in many different contexts across the curriculum.

The practical process itself is of key importance here. It is not necessary for children to record outcomes on paper, unless it enhances their learning in some way. Taking a photograph, with a digital camera ideally, is a manageable way of providing a record of the task (for inclusion in a portfolio of children's work) and evidence of the learning that has taken place.

Plants and Seeds

The children were encouraged to think about what they had learned about growing seeds.

They used a writing frame to create a series of illustrations about how best to grow seeds based on what they had learned.

Learn from experience

What have I learned?

What shall we do with this information to communicate it to others?

The children complete their 'plant growth' diaries.

Communicate

Let's tell someone

Pla

ar

see

How well did I do?

Evaluate

New knowledge gained was discussed and added to their original concept maps.

Let's do it!

Implement

The children set up an investigation and kept a 'plant growth' diary over the next three weeks.

A summary of the TASC stages involved in a project on 'Plants and Seeds'

The children brainstormed what they already knew.

They worked with their 'thinking partner' to create concept maps.

Gather/organise

What do I know about this?

nts
nd
eds

What is the task?

Identify

• To recall existing knowledge and understanding of plants and seeds.
• To identify questions to answer.
• To extend knowledge of plants and seeds, and answer questions.

How many ideas can I think of?

Generate

Which is the best idea?

Having come up with a key question they would like to find the answer to, the children generated their own ideas.

Decide

They thought about how they might find the answers to their questions.

What do we already know about this?

The children brainstormed what they already knew about plants. They worked with their 'thinking partner' to create a basic concept map of words and pictures.

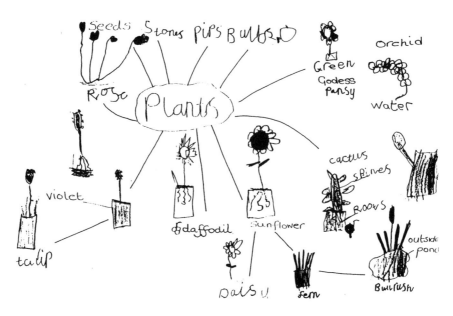

Concept map (before block of work)

What is it that we want to find out?

The teacher established clear learning objectives for the lesson. These included:

- To recall existing knowledge and understanding of plants and seeds.

- To know that there are different plants in the immediate environment.

Children generated a list of questions they wanted to answer.

Lesson focus: Plants and seeds
Concept map - accessing prior knowledge. Setting up seed growth investigation.

Year group/s: 1/2	QCA Unit links: 2b

Lesson Learning Objective:
To recall existing knowledge of plants and seeds.
To set up an investigation into what conditions seeds need to grow well.

LESSON PLAN
Introduction: Whole class
Brainstorm what children know already about plants and seeds. Model how to link ideas together in a simple concept map.
Children in pairs begin to draw a map of their own ideas (20 minutes). Give some pairs a list of words and pictures to include.

Group or individual activities:

Tell children that we are going to find out about how best to grow sunflower seeds.

Ask them a series of questions. What do we need to do? What equipment? Where should we put the seeds? etc. Discuss together and devise a method.
Set up investigation in groups - put seeds in pots in different positions.

More able - Write up report and predict about seed position and water.
Average - Use writing frame to structure investigation report. Make prediction.
Less able - Draw equipment and label. Write simple prediction (adult to record)

Plenary:
Discuss what each group has learned.

What should we do now? How might we record what happens to each pot of seeds? Draw a 'diary' on flipchart for children to use over next three weeks.

Extension / Support

See above

Resources
Pots, compost, sunflower seeds

Teacher's short-term lesson plan

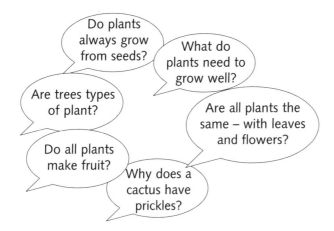

What is our question?

The children came up with a key question that they were keen to find the answer to: 'What do plants need to grow well?'

They then came up with their own ideas.

Bulb planting

> *Comment*
>
> Children should be encouraged to suggest (with guidance) how they might find the answer to their questions.
>
> Appropriate methods might be:
>
> ● Plant seeds or bulbs and keep a diary and log their growth of over time.
>
> ● Look at seed packets and gardening books for information.
>
> ● Ask an expert gardener for advice.

Let's do it!

The children set up an investigation (with support) and kept a diary of what happened to their sunflower seeds over the next three weeks. Where appropriate they recorded measurements as well as observations.

What did we find out?

The children looked at their original concept maps and added things they had learned while investigating what plants and seeds need to grow well.

How can we tell others what we've found out?

After three weeks of observing, measuring and recording, the children completed their plant growth diaries.

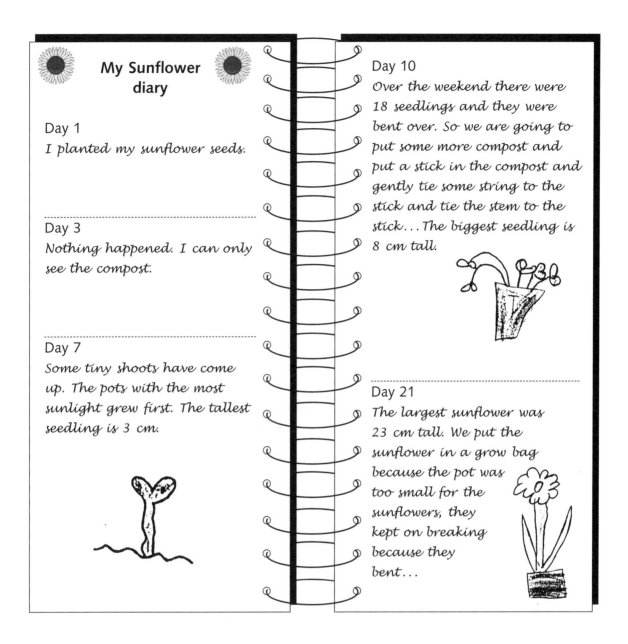

My Sunflower diary

Day 1

I planted my sunflower seeds.

Day 3

Nothing happened. I can only see the compost.

Day 7

Some tiny shoots have come up. The pots with the most sunlight grew first. The tallest seedling is 3 cm.

Day 10

Over the weekend there were 18 seedlings and they were bent over. So we are going to put some more compost and put a stick in the compost and gently tie some string to the stick and tie the stem to the stick... The biggest seedling is 8 cm tall.

Day 21

The largest sunflower was 23 cm tall. We put the sunflower in a grow bag because the pot was too small for the sunflowers, they kept on breaking because they bent...

What have we learned?

Learn from experience

Encourage the children to think about what they have learned about how to grow seeds. The children used a writing frame to create a series of instructions about how best to grow seeds based on what they had learned.

Instructions for Growing Seeds

First . . . *get some seeds and put them into some compost in a pot.*

Then . . . *put some water on the seeds - be careful not to put too much on.*

Next . . . *look after the seeds, check them every day, and give them water when they need it. They might need a stick after about ten days.*

Finally . . . *you will have a big sunflower plant, about 23 cm tall. It needs to be planted out in the garden or in a grow bag.*

We grew these ourselves

Brainstorming and mindmapping

Brainstorming and mindmapping can be used at the beginning and end of a block or unit of work. Brainstorming provides children with an opportunity to generate as many ideas as they can think of relating to a given topic. However, it is necessary for the children to make links between the 'bits' of knowledge that are generated in this way so that whole concepts are developed rather than fragmented ideas. These processes allow them not only to access prior learning but also identify when and where they need to know more. When children add to their mindmap at the end of a unit of work, evidence of progress made and learning outcomes will be revealed.

PURPOSE

How to do it

- Ask children what they know about a particular topic, for instance, rocks. Prior knowledge may originate from previous experiences in school but other sources are equally valuable, such as a TV programme about volcanoes, a parent or grandparent who is an expert gardener, a child with a collection of rocks accumulated from holiday visits to beaches. Stimulate discussion where necessary, perhaps by reading part of an entertaining information-based text, watching part of a video or discussing recent relevant science or geography work.

- Accept all of the children's ideas at this stage and note them randomly on a flip-chart.

- When sufficient words, ideas or facts have been noted, begin to highlight associated items in the same colour, e.g. 'What rocks are used for'. Although it is important to gather what the children already know, it is also necessary to group ideas so that the children can make links between them. This helps them not only to understand but also to remember ideas in meaningful clusters instead of in fragments.

- Discuss any items that do not seem to fit into a group. Either pick these up later, for example through a research task or specific activity, or discard if irrelevant (and with the agreement of the children).

- At the end of the unit of work use the same headings again and list 'what we have learned'.

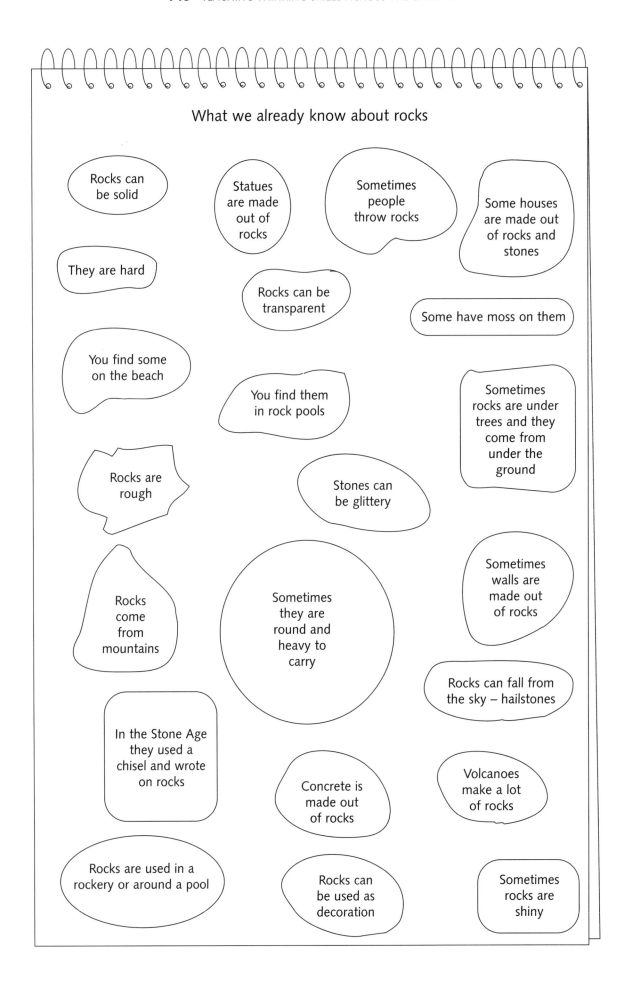

What we already know about rocks

Rocks can be solid

Statues are made out of rocks

Sometimes people throw rocks

Some houses are made out of rocks and stones

They are hard

Rocks can be transparent

Some have moss on them

You find some on the beach

You find them in rock pools

Sometimes rocks are under trees and they come from under the ground

Rocks are rough

Stones can be glittery

Rocks come from mountains

Sometimes they are round and heavy to carry

Sometimes walls are made out of rocks

Rocks can fall from the sky – hailstones

In the Stone Age they used a chisel and wrote on rocks

Concrete is made out of rocks

Volcanoes make a lot of rocks

Rocks are used in a rockery or around a pool

Rocks can be used as decoration

Sometimes rocks are shiny

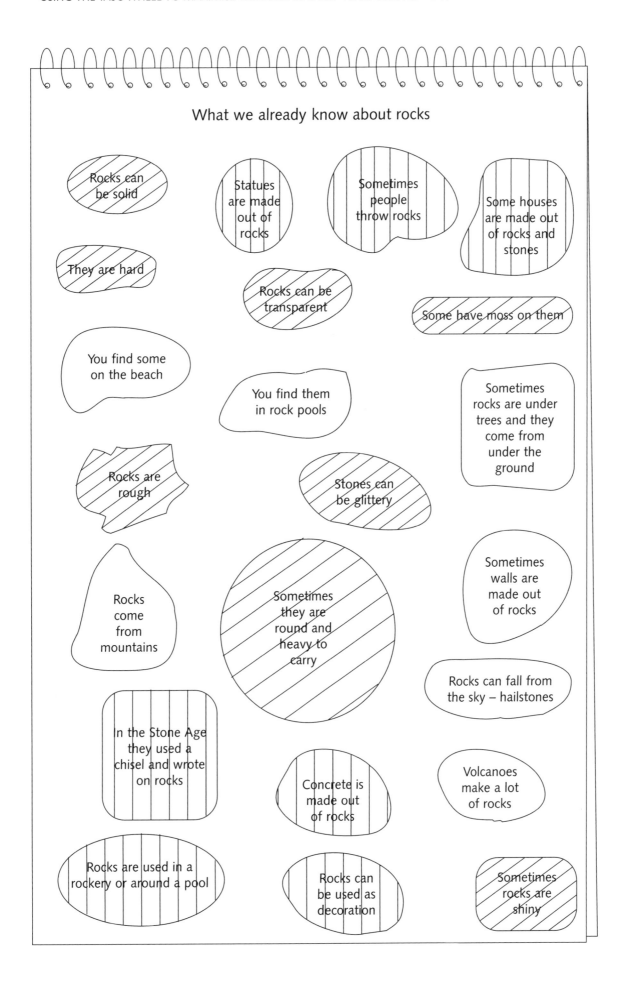

What we already know about rocks

Rocks can be solid

Statues are made out of rocks

Sometimes people throw rocks

Some houses are made out of rocks and stones

They are hard

Rocks can be transparent

Some have moss on them

You find some on the beach

You find them in rock pools

Sometimes rocks are under trees and they come from under the ground

Rocks are rough

Stones can be glittery

Sometimes walls are made out of rocks

Rocks come from mountains

Sometimes they are round and heavy to carry

Rocks can fall from the sky – hailstones

In the Stone Age they used a chisel and wrote on rocks

Concrete is made out of rocks

Volcanoes make a lot of rocks

Rocks are used in a rockery or around a pool

Rocks can be used as decoration

Sometimes rocks are shiny

REFLECT

What have we learned?

What we have learned about rocks

What they look like
Rough ➤ sea changes then ➤ smooth
Some hard – granite, marble
Some crumbly – sandstone, coal, chalk
Lots of different colours
Some have layers
Some have fossils – amber, limestone ➤ can be polished
Some have air holes – volcanic rock ➤ lava

Where they come from
Granite ➤ from volcanoes
Sandstone ➤ under the sea, get it from quarries
Lava ➤ melted rock ➤ from volcanoes
Some rocks are made from shells – limestone
Opals and amethysts come from mountains
Amber is tree resin that has been underground for millions of years
Chalk cliffs

What they are used for
Marble – statues ➤ because it can be polished
Slate – writing on ➤ because it's smooth
          roof tiles ➤ because it's waterproof and splits easily
Sandstone – buildings ➤ because it's cheap and easy to cut
Granite – under a fireplace ➤ because it's hard
Marble – buildings, but not much because it's expensive but
          hard
Marble or granite – grave stones > because they last longer

Pushes and Pulls

What do we already know about this?

The children looked at a collection of cars and discussed their ideas about how they thought the cars might move.

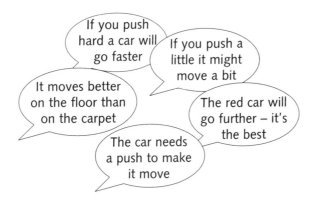

What is it that we want to find out?

The teacher established clear learning objectives for the lesson. These included:

● To know that pushes and pulls are both forces.

● To investigate a science question.

The focus for the investigation was identified as: 'Whether the surface that a car travels over makes any difference to how far or how fast it travels.'

STICKNEY CE PRIMARY SCHOOL WEEKLY PLANNING...

LEARNING OBJECTIVE	KEY VOCABULARY	WHOLE-CLASS TEACHING	LOW/MIXED ABILITY TASK	HIGH ABILITY TASK	PLENARY/ HOMEWORK	ASSESSMENT/ NEXT STEPS
ATI To investigate a given question. 2b To know that pushes and pulls are forces.	forces push pull ramp further/est slow fast low/steep	Discuss different forces (recap)	Look at ramp with toy car. Predict when the car will go furthest - with a steep ramp/with a low ramp. Try out and discuss.		Children give reasons for their findings.	Most children were able to predict where the car would end up according to how steep the ramp was. Some used vocab 'force'.
2b To know that pushes and pulls are both forces. 2a To find out about weight. ATI Investigate questions.	push pull travel ramp further furthest low/steep	Discuss last practical lesson. What did we find out?	Draw and label 3 ramps and where the cars should travel to.	Ask a question to investigate, and suggest through pictures and drawings how we would find out.	Look at children's drawings and test. Discuss questions asked by children and explain what they'll do.	Still finding it difficult to formulate and investigate questions, although can suggest ways of testing questions with prompting.

Teacher's weekly lesson plan

A summary of the TASC stages involved in a project on
'Pushes and Pulls'

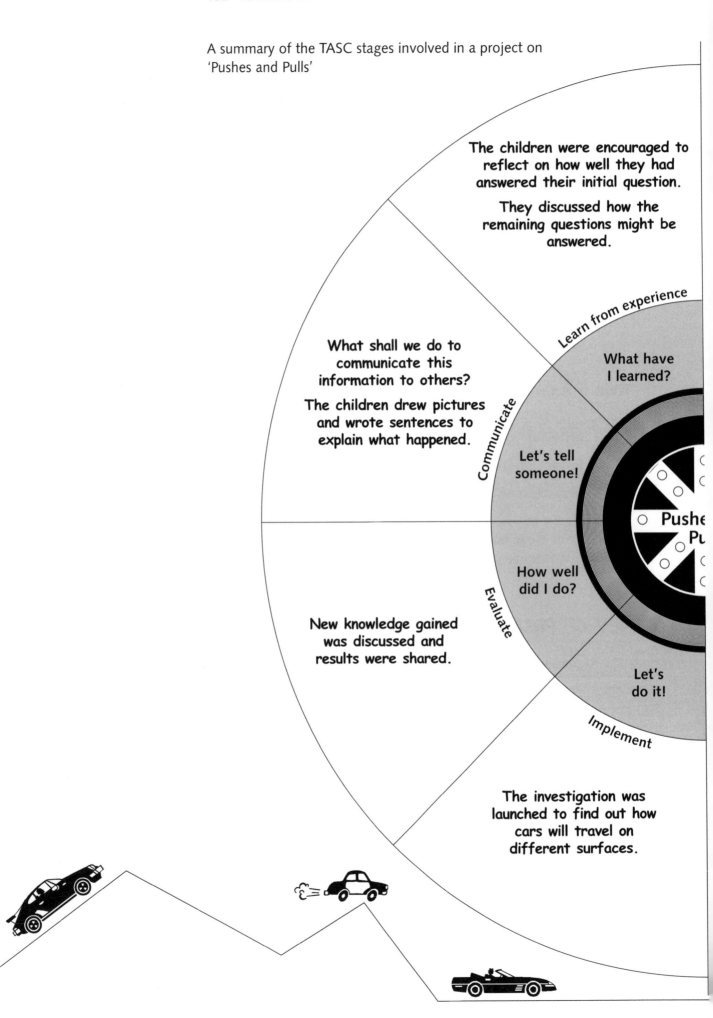

The children were encouraged to reflect on how well they had answered their initial question.

They discussed how the remaining questions might be answered.

Learn from experience

What have I learned?

What shall we do to communicate this information to others?

The children drew pictures and wrote sentences to explain what happened.

Communicate

Let's tell someone!

How well did I do?

Evaluate

New knowledge gained was discussed and results were shared.

Let's do it!

Implement

The investigation was launched to find out how cars will travel on different surfaces.

Pushe
Pu

The children brainstormed what they already knew about cars and discussed how they might move.

Gather/organise

What do I know about this?

Identify

• To know that pushes and pulls are both forces.
• To investigate a science question: 'Whether the surface that a car travels over affects its speeds.'

What is the task?

es and ılls

How many ideas can I think of?

Generate

They came up with a key question that they wanted to find the answer to.

Preparations for the investigation were made.

Which is the best idea?

Decide

The children thought about what might happen during the investigation.

What is our question?

> Will the cars go
> the same distance
> over different
> surfaces?

The surfaces to be compared were identified by the children and classified as either 'rough' or 'smooth'.

Surface	Rough or smooth?
Playground paint	*rough*
Grass	*rough*
Bark chips	*rough*
Tarmac path	*rough*
Door mat	*rough*
Cloakroom floor tiles	*smooth*
Table	*smooth*
Hall floor	*smooth*

Decide ▶ **What might happen?**

The children predicted what they thought would happen when the car was rolled onto different surfaces.

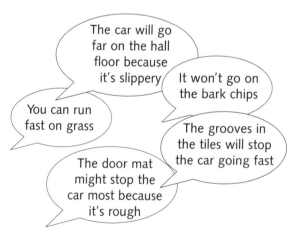

Let's do it!

Science Investigation.

We wanted to find out about how far a car will travel when it is pushed along different surfaces.

Here is a picture to show what we did:

We let the car roll down a ramp onto different surfaces. We measured the distance in straws. We made a table to show our results.

How do we control how far it rolls?

What did we find out? Did we answer our question?

Surface	Rough or Smooth?	Distance in straws
Playground paint	*rough*	*1 ³/₄*
Grass	*rough*	*0*
Bark chips	*rough*	*1*
Tarmac path	*rough*	*2*
Door mat	*rough*	*1 ³/₄*
Cloakroom floor tiles	*smooth*	*2 ¹/₂*
Table	*smooth*	*3 ¹/₂*
Hall floor	*smooth*	*2 ³/₄*

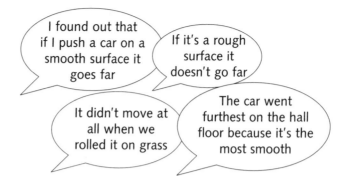

 Communicate

How can we tell others what we've found out?

The children drew pictures and wrote simple sentences to explain what happened.

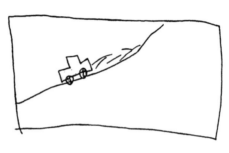

We found out:

I found out if I push a car
on a smooth surface its far. If its
rough it dónt go far.

Learn from experience

What have we learned?

The children reflected on how well they had answered their question. They identified other questions they might need to explore:

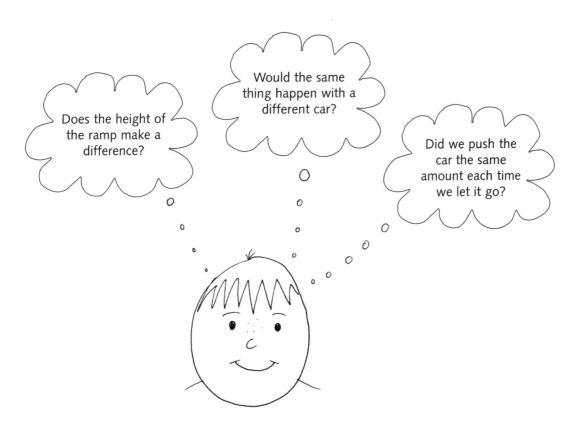

Children communicated their knowledge and understanding in a variety of ways during the course of their work on 'Pushes and Pulls'.

They produced a series of posters to communicate the need to find a safe place to cross the road and drew diagrams to explain where force must be applied to make objects around the classroom move.

K W L

What do we **Know**? What do we **Want** to find out?
What have we **Learned**?

Using a KWL approach with children involves children in think-ing that relates to several stages of the TASC Wheel.

Establishing **'What do we know?'** requires children to think about any prior knowledge and understanding they already have about a subject (Gather/organise). This 'knowledge' might emanate from school-based learning but is equally likely to be the result of everyday experiences at home, in the garden or playground.

Thinking about **'What do we want/need to find out?'** or **'What do we need to think about?'** involves children in the fundamental scientific skill of asking questions and suggesting possible answers (Decide/Generate).

NC Programme of Study reference

Sc1 2a and b: Pupils should be taught to ask questions and decide how they might find answers to them. They should use first-hand experience and simple information sources to answer questions.

As children consider **'What have we learned?'** following a topic, series of activities or an investigation, they must think about several key questions; 'Did we answer our original ques-tion/s?' 'How well did we do?' 'What else do we need to find out?' (Evaluate/Learn from experience). The process of reflection is essential if children are to crystallise what they have learned.

NC Programme of Study reference

Sc1 2j: Pupils should be taught to review their work and explain what they did to others.

How to do it

A KWL approach is particularly effective if children work collab-oratively, sharing their thoughts and ideas at every stage.

- Gather the children on the carpet with their 'thinking part-ner' sitting beside them. Initiate a discussion by asking a series of questions relating to a particular problem.

For example, ask them to think about a time when they have been given a parcel of some kind. What sort of wrapping did the parcel have? What did it look like? What did it feel like? What purpose did the wrapping have? What about a parcel that comes through the post? What does that wrapping need to be like? Ask the children to share their ideas and experiences with their thinking partner (a collection of samples of possible wrapping materials might be used as a stimulus at this point).

● Record the children's ideas on the flip-chart – accept all ideas and suggestions.

What do we know already about wrapping a parcel?

My mum uses shiny wrapping paper.

You need to stick it so that it stays.

You could use string to tie it up.

You could use thick paper and put a pattern on it.

You can use a box or big envelope to put things in.

It mustn't be see through.

It needs to be strong if it's going in the post box.

Crêpe paper or tissue wouldn't be any good.

You need to put a name on it so that it gets to the right person.

● Summarise the ideas the children have come up with, e.g. 'We've had parcels with shiny red paper', 'in a padded envelope', in a box with a label', 'We need to use sticky tape or string'.

Identify

● Set the scene for an investigation for the children to explore practically, e.g. 'We need to send a parcel through the post to Little Red Riding Hood. We're sending her a new straw sun hat (show example), so we need to think of a way to keep it safe and make sure it reaches her at her grandmother's house.'

Generate

● Ask children to discuss with their thinking partner 'What do we need to think about?' Again, record their ideas in the form of questions on a page of flip-chart.

What do we need to think about?

How can we protect the sun hat so that it doesn't get broken?

> *Use a box.*
>
> *Wrap it in paper.*
>
> *Use foam round it.*

What if it rains when the postman is delivering the parcel?

> *Use some plastic.*
>
> *Use thick paper.*
>
> *Shiny paper would be good.*

How will the postman know where to deliver the parcel?

> *Write her name on it.*
>
> *Put a label on.*
>
> *You need her address.*
>
> *The writing must not run if the parcel gets wet or she won't get it.*

● When children have completed their investigation, and as part of the process of 'considering evidence', look again at the questions identified earlier.

What have we learned?

We decided to put the sun hat in a strong cardboard box and stuff kitchen paper inside so that it won't squash.

We used plastic sheet (from a carrier bag) to wrap up the box - it won't let the wet in. We stuck it with strong tape to make sure there were no gaps.

We couldn't write on the plastic using a pen so we stuck some paper on as a label. We wrote on it using biro because it doesn't run like a felt tip pen.

Learn from experience

Our Senses

A summary of the TASC stages involved in a project on
'Our Senses'

The children reflected on
what they had learned
about their senses.

Learn from experience

What shall we do with this
information to communicate
it to others?

The children chose various
ways to record their
findings (e.g. words and
pictures)

Communicate

What have
I learned?

Let's tell
someone!

How
well
did I do?

Evaluate

Results of the
investigation were
considered and new
knowledge gained
was listed.

Let's
do it!

Implement

Three children were
selected to take part in
the investigation.

Measurements were taken
and recorded along with
observations.

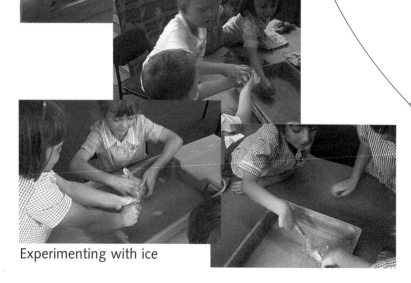

Experimenting with ice

The children brainstormed what they already knew.

They discussed their ideas with their 'thinking partner' before creating concept maps.

Gather/organise

What do I know about this?

What is the task?

Identify

- To understand and identify their five senses.
- To investigate a question about one of the senses they would like to find the answer to.

I think I'll like this one

ur
ses

How many ideas can I think of?

Generate

Which is the best idea?

A key question was chosen, based on the topic 'hearing sounds'.

The children thought about how well they could hear when their ears were covered and uncovered.

Decide

They thought about how they might find the answer to their key question.

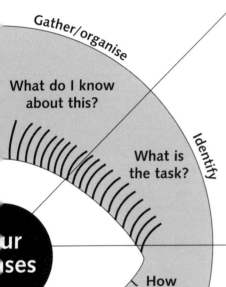

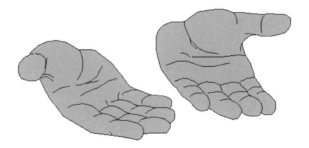

Gather & organise

What do we already know about this?

The children brainstormed what they already knew about their senses – sight, taste, hearing, smell, and touch. They worked with their 'thinking partner' to create a basic concept map of words and pictures for one of the senses.

Identify

What is it that we want to find out?

The teacher established clear learning objectives for the unit of work. These included:

● To understand and identify their five senses.

● To investigate a question about one of the senses.

Theme/Topic: Our Senses	NC Links: Ourselves Sc2g - Children should be taught about senses that enable humans and other animals to be aware of the world around them.	
Early Learning Goals: Investigate objects and materials by using all their senses as appropriate.		
Learning Objectives	**Activities**	**Vocabulary**
Children should learn: To understand and identify their five senses and how these are used in finding out about the world. To investigate a question about one of their senses.	• Brainstorm how we find out about the world around us. Identify organs used and name sense. • Concept map of sound sources. • Take a walk around the school grounds using senses to identify sounds. • Explore how we use our eyes to see. What do they help us see? E.g. shape, colour, size, position of objects. • Taste test. Present children with a number of different foods to taste. Focus on descriptive language, e.g. bitter, sharp, sweet, salty. Make generalisations about tastes they like or dislike. • Touch. Ask children to touch a range of objects and describe what they feel, e.g. temperature, texture. Record in pictures and words. • Investigation - How well can we hear with ears covered or uncovered?	Descriptive language Names of senses and organs **Resources** Sound sources Foods to taste Objects to explore by ... **Skills** Observation Comparing and classifying Description Recording
	Key Questions	**Next Steps**
	How does it look / feel / taste? Which part of our bodies do we use to...? How could we find out?	

Teacher's lesson plan

Children generated a list of questions they wanted to answer.

I'm not sure about this taste

What is our question?

Children came up with their own ideas.

How can we answer our question? What do we need to do?

The children decided how they might set up an investigation – with support from their teacher and another adult helper.

> ### *Comment*
>
> Children should be given a simple 'writing frame' that will provide them with structured support as they learn how to investigate a question. This may be copied onto paper, written as headings on a whiteboard or displayed somewhere in the classroom.
>
> For example:
>
> > What do we want to find out?
> >
> > This is what we did...
> > These are our results...
> > We learnt that...

Let's do it!

Three children were selected from the class. Others checked whether they were able to hear a chime bar each metre – from 2 m to 20 m – away from the sound source, first with ears uncovered and then wearing ear muffs. They recorded measurements as well as their observations.

Evaluate

What did we find out?

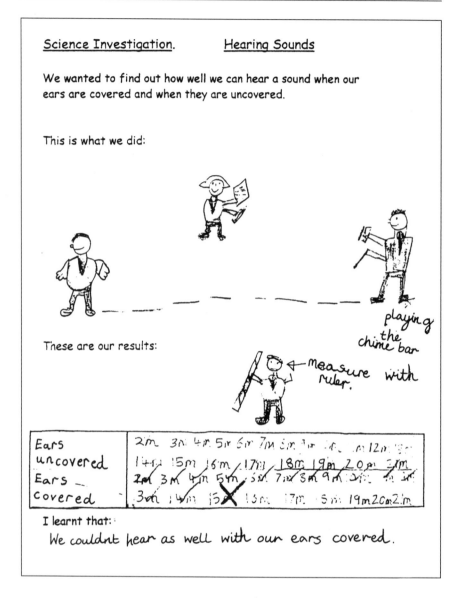

Science Investigation.   Hearing Sounds

We wanted to find out how well we can hear a sound when our ears are covered and when they are uncovered.

This is what we did:

playing the chime bar

These are our results:

measure with ruler.

Ears uncovered	2m 3m 4m 5m 6m 7m ... 12m ... 14m 15m 16m 17m 18m 19m 20m 21m
Ears covered	2m 3m 4m 5m ... 7m 8m 9m ... 3m 4m 5m 15m 17m 18m 19m 20m 21m

I learnt that:
We couldn't hear as well with our ears covered.

Communicate

How can we tell others what we've found out?

Children recorded what they had found out about all their senses in a variety of ways, using a combination of words and pictures.

green apple 'sour'

sweets 'sweet'

chilli – hot

ice-lolly-cold

salty

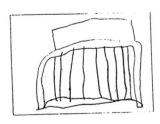

radiator – hot

silky scarf

What have we learned?

Learn from experience

The children reflected on what they had learned about their five senses. They were able to name each sense, identify the organ responsible and describe what they had found out.

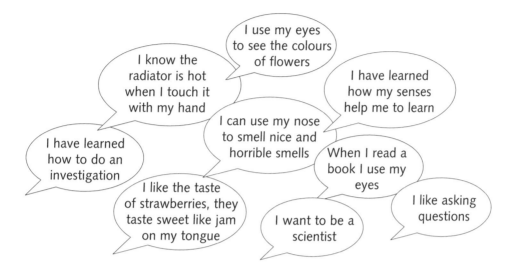

I use my eyes to see the colours of flowers

I know the radiator is hot when I touch it with my hand

I have learned how my senses help me to learn

I can use my nose to smell nice and horrible smells

I have learned how to do an investigation

When I read a book I use my eyes

I like the taste of strawberries, they taste sweet like jam on my tongue

I want to be a scientist

I like asking questions

What does my tongue look like?

What are the colours in these?

Theme/Topic:	NC Links:	
Early Learning Goals:		
Learning Objectives	**Activities**	**Vocabulary**
Children should learn:		
		Resources
		Skills
	Key Questions	**Next Steps**

Sample Early Years short-term planning sheet for science

© Belle Wallace, 2002, *Teaching Thinking Skills Across the Early Years*, David Fulton Publishers.

Bibliography and Useful Resources

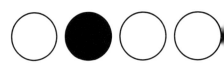

References and further reading

Adams, H. B. (1986) 'Teaching general problem-solving strategies in the classroom', *Gifted Educational International,* **4**(2), pp. 84–9.

Department for Education and Employment (DfEE) (2000) *National Literacy and Numeracy Strategies: Guidance on Teaching Able Children.* London: DfEE.

Donaldson, M. (1983) *Children's Minds.* London: Fontana Press.

Gardner, H. (1983) *Frames of Mind.* London: Fontana Press.

Holt, J. (1983) *How Children Learn.* Harmondsworth: Penguin Books.

Porter, L. (1999) *Gifted Young Children: A Guide for Teachers and Parents.* Buckingham: Open University Press.

Renzulli, J. S., Reis, S. M. and Smith, L. H. (1981) *The Revolving Door Identification Model.* Connecticut: Creative Learning Press.

Sternberg, R. J. (1985) *Beyond IQ: A Triarchic Theory of Human Intelligence.* Cambridge: Cambridge University Press.

Sternberg, R. J. and Davidson, J. E. (1986) *Conceptions of Giftedness.* Cambridge: Cambridge University Press.

Vygotsky, L. S. (1978) *Mind in Society: The Development of Higher Psychological Processes.* Cambridge, MA: Harvard University Press.

Wallace, B. (1988) 'Curriculum enrichment for all pupils then curriculum extension', *Critical Arts: A Journal for Cultural Studies,* **4**(1), pp. 4–5.

Wallace, B. (2000) *Teaching the Very Able Child: Developing a Policy and Adopting Strategies for Provision.* London: David Fulton Publishers.

Wallace, B. (2001) *Teaching Thinking Skills Across the Primary Curriculum: A Practical Approach for All Abilities.* London: David Fulton Publishers.

Wallace, B. and Adams, H. B. (1993) *TASC: Thinking Actively in a Social Context.* Oxford: AB Academic Publishers.

Literacy

Adey, P. and Shayer, M. (1994) *Really Raising Standards Cognitive Intervention and Academic Achievement*. Routledge *(Powerful arguments for the ways thinking skills can raise standards)*

Buzan, T. (2000) *The Mind Map Book*. BBC Worldwide Ltd *(Practical approaches to developing thinking using mind mapping)*

De Bono, E. (1992) *Teach your child to think*. Penguin Books *(Many practical approaches to developing thinking. Young children respond to and enjoy working with the 'thinking hats')*

Fisher, R. (1992) *Teaching Children to Think*. Stanley Thornes *(Very good background reading to the whole process of developing thinking across the curriculum, especially the chapter on 'Critical Thinking')*

Gardner, H. (1991) *The Unschooled Mind*. Fontana Press *(This book examines both the school learning environment and different approaches to learning)*

Higgins, S. (2001) *Thinking through Primary Teaching*. Chris Kington publishing *(Theoretical and practical strategies for developing thinking skills in the classroom)*

Lipman, M. (1991) *Thinking in Education*. Cambridge University Press *(Part one has an excellent overview of the importance of thinking in education)*

Murris, K. *Storywise: Thinking through stories*. Dialogue Works *(A practical approach to using stories to develop thinking skills)*

Ridings, R. and Rayner, S. (1999) *Cognitive Styles and Learning Strategies*. David Fulton Publishers *(A review of different theories about learning and practical examples of how learning styles and strategies affect the way children learn)*

Wallace, B. (2000) *Teaching the Very Able Child*. David Fulton Publishers *(A very practical book on developing and implementing a whole school policy)*

Wallace, B. (ed.) (2001) *Teaching Thinking Skills Across the Primary Curriculum: A practical approach for all abilities*. David Fulton Publishers *(Another good practical introduction to teaching thinking skills across the curriculum)*

Worcestershire Educational Services (2002) *Mixed-Age Planning: key learning and thinking skills across the primary curriculum*. *(A practical approach to planning teaching and learning across the subject range of the national curriculum using subject specific skills and thinking skills)*

Watching and Learning 2. Evaluation of the implementation of the national literacy and numeracy strategies by Ontario Institute for Studies in Education, University of Toronto, September 2001 DfES 0617/2001 *(An interesting analysis of the strategies which also reflects on the place of thinking skills in the national curriculum)*.

Numeracy

Atkinson, S. (1992) *Mathematics with Reason: The Emergent Approach to Primary Maths*. London: Hodder and Stoughton.

Atkinson, S., Harrison, S. and McClure, L. (1996) *New Cambridge Primary Maths Modules 1, 2, 3*. Cambridge: Cambridge University Press.

Carraher, T. N., Carrehar, D. W. and Schliemann, A. D. (1991) 'Mathematics in the streets and in schools', in P. Light, S. Sheldon and M. Woodhead (eds) *Learning to Think*. London: Routledge.

Eyre, D. and McClure, L. (eds) *Curriculum Provision for the Gifted and Talented in the Primary School*. London: David Fulton Publishers.

Office for Standards in Education (OFSTED) (1994) *Improving Schools*. London: The Stationery Office.

Pohl, M. (1997) *Teaching Thinking Skills in the Primary Years*. Melbourne: Hawker Brownlow Education.

Polya, G. (1957) *How to solve it* (2nd edn). New Jersey: Princeton University Press.

Pound, L. (1999) *Supporting Mathematical Development in the Early Years*. Buckingham: Open University Press.

Qualifications and Curriculum Authority (QCA)/Department for Education and Employment (DfEE) (2000) *Curriculum Guidance for the Foundation Stage.* London: QCA/DfEE.

Skemp, R. R. (1989) *Mathematics in the Primary School.* London: Routledge.

Thumpston, G. (1994) 'Mathematics in the National Curriculum: implications for learning in the early years', in G. Blenkin and A. V. Kelly (eds) *The National Curriculum and Early Learning.* London: Paul Chapman.

Websites of interest

Association of Teachers of Mathematics (ATM)
    www.atm.org.uk
Coolmaths (American fun maths site)
    www.coolmath.com/
Hoagies gifted and talented site (American site with lots of links)
    www.hoagieskids.org/kidsMnS.htm
The Mathematical Association (MA)
    www.m-a.org.uk/
Maths Year 2000/Counton
    http://Mathsyear.2000.org
MEP Mathematics Enhancement Programme (Resources from Exeter University)
    www.ex.ac.uk
NRICH (Online maths enrichment club of Cambridge University. A vast resource for pupils, parents and teachers. Not to be missed!)
    http://nrich.maths.org.uk
Royal Institution of Great Britain (RI) (Information about primary maths and science lectures in London and other areas, and masterclass networks)
    www.ri.ac.uk/

Science

Banks, H. and Handsley, S. (1998) *Knowledge and Understanding of the World.* Leamington Spa: Scholastic.

Beasley, G. and Pengelly, B. (1999) *Further Curriculum Bank Activities: Science Key Stage 1.* Leamington Spa: Scholastic.

Garnett, S. (1997) *The Home Corner*, Learning Through Play series. Leamington Spa: Scholastic.

Harpley, A. and Roberts, A. (1997) *Sand*, Learning Through Play series. Leamington Spa: Scholastic.

Harpley, A. and Roberts, A. (1997) *Water*, Learning Through Play series. Leamington Spa: Scholastic.

Kings, T. (1997) *Learning Through Story: Science.* Dunstable: Folens.

Naylor, B. and Naylor, S. (2000) *The Snowman's Coat and Other Science Questions.* London: Hodder Children's Books.

Northampton Inspection and Advisory Service (NIAS) (1998) Early Years Science Resources: *All Sorts of Stuff; Big Beasts, Little Beasts; Pottering with Plants* and *You, Me and Us.* Northampton: NIAS.

Index